Kangaroos Behind Bars

Kangaroos Behind Bars

Navigating Captive Environments

Sam Loray

Spectra Enterprise

CONTENTS

INDEX

Introduction

INTRODUCTION

Kangaroos, famous images of the Australian outback, exemplify the soul of the wild with their limitless energy and special marsupial appeal. Nonetheless, as our reality goes through quick changes driven by urbanization, natural surroundings misfortune, and ecological changes, the difficulties looked by kangaroo populaces have incited a nearer assessment of their preservation and the board procedures. One feature of this investigation digs into the mind boggling universe of hostage conditions, where kangaroos wind up in the slammer, provoking basic investigations into their government assistance, preservation suggestions, and the moral elements of their imprisonment.

In the tremendous and different scenes of Australia, kangaroos have flourished for a long period of time, finely tuned to the rhythms of nature. However, as human exercises keep on molding the climate, the crossing point of kangaroos with human settlements has become progressively perplexing. This intricacy is enhanced by the requirement for protection mediations to shield kangaroo populaces confronting dangers, for example, territory discontinuity, environmental change, and human-natural life clashes. Inside this unique situation, the idea of "Kangaroos In the slammer" typifies the diverse truth of kangaroos exploring hostage conditions, whether in zoos, safe-havens, or untamed life parks.

1. **The Reason for "Kangaroos In the slammer"**
   This investigation, crossing the domains of science, protection science, morals, and public commitment, looks to disentangle the layers of importance and challenge related with kangaroos in bondage. "Kangaroos In a correctional facility" isn't just an unmistakable expression yet a focal point through which we look at the different elements of kangaroo the board, from the moral contemplations of imprisonment to the complexities of protection inside bound spaces. By exploring this landscape, we plan to cultivate an exhaustive comprehension of the job and effect of hostage conditions on kangaroos, with a focal point zeroed

in on their government assistance, conduct respectability, preservation esteem, and the moral obligations related with their consideration.

2. **The Development of Human-Kangaroo Communications**

The connection among people and kangaroos is old and complex, established in the scenes that the two species call home. Native Australians have imparted this land to kangaroos for millennia, winding around social stories and environmental information that profoundly interface them to these marsupials. Nonetheless, as European settlement unfurled, modifying the scene and elements of the biological system, the connection among kangaroos and people changed.

Today, kangaroos not just possess the immense stretches of the Australian wild yet in addition experience human-overwhelmed spaces, prompting difficulties and open doors in dealing with this concurrence.

3. **Protection Objectives and Moral Issues**

The basic for kangaroo protection emerges from the complicated dance between saving biodiversity, keeping up with biological equilibrium, and shielding an animal varieties symbolic of Australia's personality. In any case, as preservation techniques unfurl, moral difficulties surface, especially with regards to hostage conditions. Inquiries concerning the moral treatment of individual kangaroos, the effect of imprisonment on their prosperity, and the harmony between preservation objectives and moral contemplations become central. It is inside these problems that "Kangaroos In jail" fills in as a figurative entrance, welcoming us to examine the moral components of hostage the executives while simultaneously tending to the preservation challenges looked by wild kangaroo populaces.

4. **The Extension and Design of Investigation**

This investigation is organized as an exhaustive excursion into the different features of "Kangaroos In the slammer," every part disentangling a layer of the perplexing embroidery that characterizes the existences of kangaroos in bondage. According to verifiable points of view to the development of hostage nooks, wellbeing and government assistance contemplations, and the job of hostage kangaroos as envoys for protection, this investigation plans to give a nuanced and adjusted point of view. It dives into the difficulties, advancements, moral contemplations, and future bearings that shape the scene of kangaroo the board in hostage conditions.

5. **Connecting Science, Morals, and Public Commitment**

The investigation of "Kangaroos In a correctional facility" spans the domains of science, morals, and public commitment. It combines logical exploration on kangaroo science and conduct with moral systems that guide their administration in imprisonment. Besides, perceiving the significance of public mindfulness and contribution, this investigation investigates the job of hostage kangaroos in training, outreach, and as envoys for natural life protection. By encouraging a comprehensive getting it, we try to add to informed talk, moral independent direction, and a common obligation to the prosperity and preservation of kangaroos.

In the parts that follow, we set out on an excursion that navigates the scenes where kangaroos, both wild and hostage, leave their permanent pawprints. "Kangaroos In the slammer" welcomes perusers to think about the intricacies, challenges, and moral contemplations implanted in the connection point among kangaroos and the conditions that people have formed.

An excursion unfurls the story of kangaroos exploring the many-sided dance among bondage and preservation, offering experiences that motivate an aggregate liability to safeguard the regular legacy encapsulated by these wonderful marsupials.

1. Definition of Captive Environments

The expression "hostage conditions" envelops an expansive range of settings where untamed life, including different species like kangaroos, ends up under human consideration. These conditions are intended to meet different goals, going from preservation and examination to training and public commitment. Understanding the subtleties and ramifications of hostage conditions is fundamental as it shapes the prosperity of the creatures inside them and impacts more extensive preservation endeavors. In this investigation, we dive into the multi-layered meaning of hostage conditions, investigating the specific situations, purposes, challenges, and moral contemplations that encompass their reality.

II. The Setting of Hostage Conditions

1. Zoos and Natural life Parks

Zoos and natural life parks address quintessential instances of hostage conditions. These controlled settings plan to reproduce regular natural surroundings while giving a safe and oversaw space for creatures. Zoos, specifically, have advanced over the long run, changing from simple shows to centers for preservation, instruction, and exploration. Natural life parks, frequently extensive regions devoted to local or outlandish species, share comparative objectives yet may vary in their ways to deal with fenced in area plan and guest encounters.

2. Safe-havens and Recovery Focuses

Untamed life safe-havens and recovery focuses take care of creatures that require particular consideration because of wounds, orphanhood, or different elements. Safe-havens center around giving deep rooted care, focusing on the prosperity of individual creatures. Recovery focuses, then again, plan to get ready creatures for inevitable delivery back into nature. Both assume significant parts in the more extensive scene of hostage conditions, offering specific consideration customized to the requirements of their occupants.

3. Aquariums and Marine Parks

Hostage conditions reach out past earthbound settings to incorporate sea-going natural surroundings, for example, aquariums and marine parks. These conditions grandstand marine life, offering instructive open doors and bringing issues to light about the significance of sea protection.

While they give a brief look into submerged biological systems, moral contemplations emerge concerning the prosperity of marine species in bondage, given the intricacies of recreating their regular habitats.

III. Purposes and Targets

1. **Protection and Rearing Projects**

   One of the main roles of hostage conditions is to add to species protection through rearing projects. Hostage reproducing attempts mean to keep up with hereditary variety, forestall the eradication of imperiled species, and act as supplies for expected renewed introductions into nature. The outcome of reproducing programs is estimated by populace numbers as well as by the conduct and hereditary strength of people inside bondage.

2. **Research and Logical Progressions**

   Hostage conditions give controlled settings to logical examination, permitting scientists to concentrate on creature conduct, physiology, and wellbeing in manners frequently impossible in nature. Experiences acquired from hostage studies add to more extensive logical information, illuminating preservation procedures and natural life the executives rehearses. The cooperative endeavors between specialists, guardians, and establishments upgrade how we might interpret species-explicit necessities and prerequisites.

3. **Instruction and Public Mindfulness**

   Instruction and public mindfulness address significant targets of numerous hostage conditions. Zoos, safe-havens, and aquariums act as living study halls, offering guests a potential chance to interface with untamed life and gain a more profound comprehension of biodiversity and protection challenges. Very much planned instructive projects cultivate sympathy, impart a feeling of obligation, and motivate people in the future to take part in natural life protection.

4. **Recovery and Delivery**

For untamed life safe-havens and recovery focuses, the essential goal is much of the time the prosperity and possible arrival of creatures. Whether giving long lasting consideration to those unsatisfactory for discharge or restoring people for a re-visitation of the wild, these conditions assume a urgent part in moderating the effects of human-natural life clashes, wounds, or orphanhood.

IV. Challenges in Hostage Conditions

1. **Walled in area Plan and Conduct Contemplations**
   Establishing conditions that balance the requirement for wellbeing, wellbeing, and normal ways of behaving represents a huge test in hostage settings. The plan of nooks should consider the species' conduct collection, guaranteeing that creatures have potential open doors for investigation, social associations, and mental excitement. Meeting these models is especially intricate for species with broad home reaches, like kangaroos.

2. **Wellbeing and Government assistance**
   Guaranteeing the wellbeing and government assistance of creatures in imprisonment is a persistent test. Issues like pressure, stoutness, and conduct anomalies can emerge, requiring watchful checking, improvement projects, and veterinary consideration. Finding some kind of harmony between forestalling medical problems and considering regular ways of behaving is a sensitive undertaking that requires skill and a profound comprehension of every species' novel necessities.

3. **Hereditary Contemplations and Inbreeding**
   Keeping up with hereditary variety inside hostage populaces is fundamental for the drawn out progress of preservation rearing projects. Nonetheless, the test emerges while overseeing little populaces, as the gamble of inbreeding increments. Hereditary contemplations request cautious preparation, joint effort among foundations, and, at times, the acquaintance of new people with broaden the genetic stock.

4. **Moral Problems and Public Insight**

Hostage conditions frequently face moral problems, igniting banters about the ethical ramifications of restricting creatures for different purposes. Public discernment assumes an essential part in molding these discussions, with worries going from creature government assistance and the effect of imprisonment on normal ways of behaving to the need of protection rearing and the job of bondage in species safeguarding.

V. Moral Contemplations in Hostage Conditions

1. **Adjusting Preservation and Creature Government assistance**
   A focal moral issue rotates around the harmony between preservation targets and the government assistance of individual creatures. Finding some kind of harmony requires cautious thought of the moral ramifications of imprisonment, the personal satisfaction for hostage creatures, and the possible commitments of hostage conditions to more extensive preservation objectives.

2. **Straightforwardness and Instruction**
   Moral hostage the board requires straightforwardness in tasks and a promise to state funded schooling. Giving guests precise data about the motivation of bondage, preservation drives, and the difficulties looked by species in the

wild cultivates educated and sympathetic commitment. Moral organizations effectively add to preservation endeavors and offer their insight with people in general.

3. **Support for Normal Ways of behaving**

Regarding the regular ways of behaving of creatures in imprisonment is a basic moral thought. Conditions ought to be intended to consider species-common ways of behaving, whether it includes scrounging, social associations, or regional ways of behaving. Backing for normal ways of behaving adds to the mental prosperity of hostage creatures.

4. **Renewed introduction Morals**

For conditions associated with recovery and delivery, moral contemplations reach out to the course of renewed introduction. Guaranteeing that people are sufficiently ready for life in the wild, limiting human engraving, and evaluating the biological effect of renewed introductions are fundamental parts of mindful natural life restoration.

VI. Future Bearings and Advancements

1. **Mechanical Progressions**

The eventual fate of hostage conditions is interwoven with mechanical advancements that improve creature care and the board. From cutting edge observing frameworks and natural sensors to computer generated reality encounters for improvement, innovation holds the possibility to reform hostage conditions, tending to difficulties and refining the moral scene.

2. **Coordinated effort and Worldwide Drives**

Coordinated effort between foundations, preservation associations, and states on a worldwide scale is pivotal for the progress of hostage conditions. Laying out normalized rules, sharing accepted procedures, and taking part in composed rearing projects add to the aggregate effect of hostage the executives on worldwide biodiversity.

3. **Coordination of Native Information**

Perceiving and coordinating Native information and viewpoints in hostage the executives is a future bearing with moral and social importance. Native people group frequently have significant bits of knowledge into natural life conduct, environment the board, and the social significance of explicit species. Cooperative organizations can enhance hostage the executives practices and cultivate social awareness.

4. **Promotion for Economical Practices**

The fate of hostage conditions depends on a promise to feasible practices. This includes focusing on natural supportability in walled in area configuration, limiting the environmental impression of hostage offices, and pushing for preservation rehearses that add to the general soundness of biological systems.

B. Purpose of Captivity for Kangaroos

The reason for imprisonment for kangaroos, significant marsupials of the Australian outback, ranges a range of goals that interweave preservation, schooling, and moral contemplations. As human-untamed life communications develop and natural difficulties continue, the job of hostage conditions in protecting kangaroo populaces and cultivating public mindfulness turns out to be progressively critical. This investigation digs into the diverse purposes that drive the bondage of kangaroos, analyzing the protection goals, instructive open doors, and moral contemplations that shape their presence in zoos, safe-havens, and other hostage settings.

II. Protection Targets

1. **Hereditary Variety and Rearing Projects**

   One of the essential protection reasons for keeping kangaroos in bondage is the conservation of hereditary variety. Hostage conditions, for example, very much oversaw zoos and reproducing programs, assume a critical part in keeping up with practical populaces of kangaroos. Via cautiously choosing reproducing matches and overseeing hereditary variety, these projects add to the drawn out endurance and hereditary soundness of the species.

2. **Jeopardized Species and Populace The executives**

   For specific kangaroo species confronting the danger of peril, imprisonment turns into an essential device for populace the executives. Preservation rearing projects center around expanding populace numbers and laying out confirmation populaces that act as a hereditary repository. This is especially significant for species whose wild populaces are lessening because of living space misfortune, human-untamed life struggle, or different dangers.

3. **Research and Logical Experiences**

Hostage conditions give a controlled setting to logical examination on kangaroo science, conduct, and wellbeing. Specialists can lead concentrates on that may be testing or unimaginable in the wild, yielding important bits of knowledge into the species. The information acquired adds to more extensive preservation endeavors by illuminating procedures for territory security, natural life the executives, and the relief of dangers in nature.

III. Instructive Targets

1. **Public Mindfulness and Commitment**

   Bondage fills in as a strong stage for raising public mindfulness about kangaroos and their job in biological systems. Zoos, safe-havens, and instructive organizations utilize hostage kangaroo displays to draw in guests, cultivating an association between the general population and natural life. Through instructive projects, interpretive showcases, and intelligent encounters, bondage turns into a channel for imparting appreciation, compassion, and comprehension of kangaroos.

2. **Protection Informing and Promotion**

Hostage conditions frequently influence their impact to pass on significant protection messages. Guests to zoos and untamed life safe-havens are given data about the difficulties confronting kangaroos in the wild, for example, territory misfortune, environmental change, and human effects. By filling in as ministers for their wild partners, hostage kangaroos add to promotion endeavors that try to address more extensive protection issues.

3. **Research and Instructive Projects**

Instructive projects led inside hostage conditions offer open doors for top to bottom finding out about kangaroo science, environment, and preservation. These projects main interest groups, everything being equal, from schoolchildren to grown-ups, giving a stage to scattering precise data, dispersing legends, and encouraging a feeling of obligation toward natural life and the climate.

IV. Moral Contemplations

1. **Government assistance and Personal satisfaction**

A fundamental thought in the motivation behind bondage for kangaroos is guaranteeing their government assistance and giving a top notch of life. Moral establishments focus on the physical and mental prosperity of individual kangaroos, addressing concerns connected with walled in area plan, advancement, veterinary consideration, and social elements inside hostage gatherings.

2. **Species-Explicit Necessities**

Perceiving and obliging the species-explicit necessities of kangaroos is a moral objective. Kangaroos are remarkable marsupials with unmistakable ways of behaving, dietary prerequisites, and social designs. Hostage conditions should be intended to meet these particular necessities, permitting kangaroos to communicate normal ways of behaving, participate in friendly connections, and keep a degree of independence intelligent of their wild partners.

3. **Straightforwardness and Guest Schooling**

Moral bondage includes straightforwardness in activities and correspondence with guests. Moral establishments give clear data about the motivations of imprisonment, protection drives, and the difficulties looked by kangaroos in nature. Taught and informed guests are bound to see the value in the intricacies of untamed life the executives and become advocates for moral and mindful practices.

V. Challenges in Imprisonment for Kangaroos

1. **Fenced in area Plan and Space Prerequisites**
   One of the essential difficulties in hostage conditions is planning fenced in areas that balance the spatial necessities of kangaroos with the limits of imprisonment. Kangaroos are known for their enormous home ranges, and duplicating such broad conditions inside hostage settings can strategically challenge. Finding some kind of harmony between giving sufficient room and guaranteeing reasonability is quite difficult for overseers.

2. **Social Elements and Gathering Organization**
   Kangaroos are social creatures with complex social designs. Establishing viable gatherings inside hostage conditions requires cautious thought of individual characters, age, and orientation elements. Clashes can emerge, influencing the prosperity of people inside a gathering. Overseeing social elements and guaranteeing the arrangement of firm gatherings are progressing difficulties.

3. **Wellbeing The executives and Preventive Consideration**

Keeping up with the wellbeing of kangaroos in bondage includes cautious checking, preventive consideration, and responsive veterinary mediations. Wellbeing difficulties, for example, stress-related issues, heftiness, and parasitic diseases can arise, requiring a far reaching wellbeing the executives program. Moral establishments focus on proactive medical care to guarantee the prosperity of hostage kangaroos.

VI. Future Headings and Advancements

1. **High level Nook Plan**
   Future bearings in bondage for kangaroos include headways in fenced in area plan that mean to actually reproduce common habitats more. This incorporates the joining of creative highlights like regular vegetation, shifted geology, and tactile enhancement components. Mechanical developments may likewise assume a part in establishing dynamic and intuitive conditions.

2. **Cooperative Protection Drives**
   The fate of bondage for kangaroos lies in cooperative protection drives that include associations between establishments, legislative bodies, and preservation associations. Laying out normalized rules, sharing accepted procedures, and taking part in composed rearing and renewed introduction programs add to the aggregate effect of hostage the executives on worldwide biodiversity.

3. **All encompassing Wellbeing and Government assistance Projects**

Progressions in comprehensive wellbeing and government assistance projects will focus on the general prosperity of kangaroos in bondage. This incorporates customized improvement plans, conduct observing frameworks, and veterinary consideration that line up with the species-explicit necessities of individual kangaroos. All encompassing methodologies consider the physical, mental, and social parts of prosperity.

C. Ethical Considerations and Debates

The moral contemplations encompassing hostage kangaroo the executives are at the front of discussions that length protection, government assistance, and public commitment. As kangaroos wind up in different hostage conditions, including zoos, safe-havens, and recovery focuses, inquiries concerning the ethical quality of their bondage, the harmony between protection objectives and individual government assistance, and the effect of human mediations on wild populaces flash nuanced and frequently argumentative conversations. This investigation dives into the moral contemplations and discussions that shape the scene of hostage kangaroo the executives.

II. The Morals of Hostage Kangaroo The executives

1. **Adjusting Preservation and Government assistance**

   A focal moral issue in hostage kangaroo the executives rotates around the pressure between preservation objectives and individual government assistance. While protection endeavors intend to defend species and environments, moral contemplations request a cautious assessment of the effect of imprisonment on the prosperity of individual kangaroos. Adjusting these targets requires straightforward independent direction, informed by logical proof and a promise to focusing on the government assistance of every hostage person.

2. **Regard for Normal Ways of behaving**

   Moral kangaroo the board requires a significant regard for the normal ways of behaving of these marsupials. Kangaroos are adjusted to colossal developments, social associations, and explicit dietary necessities.

   Hostage conditions should be intended to consider species-common ways of behaving, offering valuable open doors for brushing, jumping, and mingling. Upholding for normal ways of behaving adds to the mental prosperity of hostage kangaroos and lines up with moral standards.

3. **Straightforwardness and Guest Instruction**

   Guaranteeing straightforwardness in hostage tasks and giving exact data to guests are moral goals. Moral establishments effectively participate in teaching the general population about the motivation behind bondage, the difficulties looked by kangaroos in the wild, and the commitments of hostage conditions to protection. Informed guests are bound to see the value in the intricacies of natural life the board and become advocates for moral practices.

4. **Joint effort with Native Points of view**

Perceiving and teaming up with Native points of view is a moral aspect that recognizes the social significance and conventional biological information held by Native people group. Coordinating Native viewpoints into hostage kangaroo the board exhibits social responsiveness and improves the moral contemplations related with preservation rehearses. Joint effort with Native people group cultivates an all encompassing methodology that values both social legacy and natural life conservation.

III. Banters in Hostage Kangaroo The executives

1. **Imprisonment and Regular Independence**

    One of the key discussions focuses on the degree to which imprisonment compromises the regular independence of kangaroos. Pundits contend that even all around planned fenced in areas can't completely repeat the extensive scenes these marsupials possess in nature. They fight that imprisonment intrinsically restricts the opportunity of development and normal ways of behaving fundamental for the prosperity of kangaroos.

2. **Protection Viability versus Individual Prosperity**

    Discusses emerge concerning the viability of hostage rearing projects for preservation purposes contrasted with the prosperity of individual kangaroos in bondage. While reproducing programs add to hereditary variety and species safeguarding, pundits question whether the advantages for the more extensive populace legitimize the likely splits the difference to the personal satisfaction experienced by people inside hostage settings.

3. **Renewed introduction Difficulties**

    The achievability and morals of once again introducing kangaroos into the wild after imprisonment address another combative discussion. Challenges incorporate the likely loss of fundamental wild ways of behaving, expanded weakness to predation, and the mental pressure related with progressing from bondage to nature. This discussion mirrors the more extensive inquiry of whether hostage conditions can satisfactorily get ready people for life right at home.

4. **Public Insight and Moral Predicaments**

The moral contemplations of hostage kangaroo the executives are entwined with public discernment. Unique perspectives among people in general add to moral issues. Some contend that bondage, when very much made due, fills essential protection and instructive needs. Others battle that the intrinsic constraints of bondage compromise the moral honesty of such endeavors. Exploring these clashing points of view is a continuous test in the moral talk encompassing hostage kangaroo the executives.

IV. Future Headings in Moral Kangaroo The board

1. **Moral Rules and Guidelines**

    The fate of moral kangaroo the executives includes the foundation of clear rules and principles. Creating moral structures that address the assorted necessities of kangaroos in imprisonment requires joint effort between preservationists, creature government assistance specialists, and ethicists. Moral rules can give an establishment to independent direction and guarantee that the prosperity of individual kangaroos stays a need.

2. **Progresses in Fenced in area Plan**

Developments in nook configuration address a promising road for tending to moral worries. Future nooks might consolidate trend setting innovations, ecological enhancement highlights, and versatile plans that better repeat regular scenes. These advancements mean to upgrade the prosperity of kangaroos in bondage and give amazing open doors to additional regular ways of behaving.

3. **Research on Mental Prosperity**

Headways in research on the mental prosperity of kangaroos in bondage add to moral contemplations. Understanding the mental and close to home requirements of kangaroos illuminates the plan regarding improvement programs, social elements inside hostage gatherings, and in general techniques for advancing positive emotional well-being. Continuous exploration endeavors are critical for refining moral practices in kangaroo the executives.

4. **Public Commitment and Backing**

Public commitment and backing are vital to forming moral practices in kangaroo the executives. Foundations focused on moral guidelines effectively include the general population in conversations about the reason for bondage, protection drives, and the difficulties looked by kangaroos. Public help for moral practices turns into a main thrust for positive change in the treatment of kangaroos in bondage.

Chapter 1

The Kangaroo In The Wild

The kangaroo, a famous image of Australia's interesting natural life, is a marsupial prestigious for its particular jumping headway and strong rear legs. In the tremendous and various scenes of Australia, kangaroos possess a scope of biological systems, exhibiting flexibility and strength. This investigation of the kangaroo in the wild digs into their regular living space, conduct, and the urgent job they play in keeping up with biological equilibrium.

Environment Variety:

Kangaroos are profoundly versatile animals, populating different conditions across Australia. From bone-dry deserts to waterfront timberlands and fields, kangaroos have shown their capacity to flourish in assorted natural surroundings. Their circulation is affected by elements, for example, food accessibility, water sources, and vegetation cover, exhibiting the kangaroo's versatility to various natural specialties.

Standards of conduct:

The way of behaving of kangaroos is impacted by their social construction, mating propensities, and taking care of inclinations. Kangaroos are for the most part friendly creatures, framing bunches known as crowds or troops. Inside these gatherings, a prevailing male, known as the "extremely confident man," frequently leads and safeguards the gathering. Females and their posterity make up most of the horde, encouraging a feeling of local area among these marsupials.

Taking care of and Rummaging:

Kangaroos are herbivores, fundamentally munching on an assortment of vegetation like grasses, bushes, and leaves. Their particular stomach related framework permits them to remove supplements from stringy plant material proficiently. The kangaroo's taking care of conduct is critical to the environment, as they assist with controlling plant development and forestall overgrazing in their territories.

Nighttime and Crepuscular Action:

Kangaroos are known for their crepuscular and nighttime exercises, meaning they are generally dynamic during day break and sunset or during the evening. This conduct is believed to be a variation to the bone-dry and hot states of numerous Australian areas, permitting kangaroos to stay away from the extraordinary intensity of the day.

Regenerative Procedures:

Kangaroos display interesting regenerative techniques, with females having two uteri and the capacity to postpone the improvement of an undeveloped organism until natural circumstances are good. This transformation guarantees that youthful kangaroos, known as joeys, have a higher opportunity of endurance once conceived. The pocket, a particular element of marsupials, gives a safeguarded climate to the lacking youthful.

Horde Elements:

The social construction of kangaroo hordes is complicated, including correspondence through vocalizations, non-verbal communication, and actual cooperations. Hordes go about as an emotionally supportive network, giving insurance against hunters and working with the sharing of assets. The progressive idea of kangaroo social orders keeps everything under control inside the gathering.

Hunters and Dangers:

Regardless of their solid rear legs and speed, kangaroos face predation from different sources. Normal hunters incorporate dingoes, birds, and enormous reptiles. Human-instigated dangers, like living space annihilation, vehicle impacts, and hunting, additionally present critical dangers to kangaroo populaces.

Biological system Architects:

Kangaroos assume an indispensable part as environment engineers, impacting vegetation design and circulation through their taking care of propensities. By specifically brushing on specific plants, kangaroos shape the scene and add to the general biodiversity of their living spaces. This effect is especially critical in bone-dry locales where vegetation is scanty.

Water Reliance:

While kangaroos are adjusted to parched conditions, they actually expect water to get by. They can get a portion of their water needs from the dampness content of the vegetation they polish off, yet they likewise depend on normal water sources like streams, lakes, and waterholes.

Transitory Way of behaving:

Some kangaroo species display transitory way of behaving, getting across huge distances looking for food and water. This itinerant way of life is a reaction to the unusual and variable states of the Australian scene, permitting kangaroos to adjust to changing ecological elements.

Influence on Native Culture:

Kangaroos hold social importance for Native Australian people group, highlighting conspicuously in Dreamtime stories and customary workmanship. The connection between native individuals and kangaroos stretches out past old stories, as these creatures have been a wellspring of food, dress, and devices for Native people group for millennia.

Protection Status:

While kangaroos are not at present delegated jeopardized, a few animal groups face confined dangers and populace declines because of environment misfortune, human exercises, and environmental change. Protection endeavors center around saving their normal living spaces and tending to the difficulties they experience in an undeniably human-ruled scene.

Research and Logical Commitments:

The kangaroo's exceptional science and conduct have made them subjects of broad logical examination. Concentrates on their regenerative physiology, social elements, and biological effect add to our more extensive comprehension of marsupials and have suggestions for natural life the board and preservation.

Communication with Different Species:

Kangaroos share their environments with a different cluster of natural life, from more modest marsupials to reptiles and birds. The associations among kangaroos and different species add to the complex trap of natural connections in Australia's environments.

Environment Transformations:

Kangaroos have developed explicit variations to adapt to Australia's difficult climatic circumstances. Their proficient thermoregulation systems, including licking their forelimbs to cool themselves, empower them to flourish in both hot and cold conditions.

Human-Natural life Struggle:

As human populaces extend and infringe upon regular living spaces, clashes among kangaroos and people can emerge. Issues like vehicle impacts, harm to rural yields, and contest for assets feature the difficulties of conjunction.

The travel industry and Social Importance:

Kangaroos are a significant fascination for untamed life the travel industry in Australia, drawing guests from around the world. Their social importance and extraordinary ways of behaving make them a point of convergence for eco-the travel industry drives, adding to neighborhood economies.

Variations to Bone-dry Conditions:

In dry locales, where water is scant, kangaroos have created transformations to limit water misfortune. Their concentrated pee and proficient kidney capability are instances of physiological highlights that assist them with flourishing in water-scant conditions.

Job in Seed Dispersal:

Kangaroos coincidentally add to seed dispersal as they get across scenes. Seeds from the plants they consume can be shipped in their excrement, helping with the recovery of vegetation and impacting plant dissemination.

1.1 Natural Habitat and Behavior

The normal environment and conduct of kangaroos are inherently connected to the assorted scenes of Australia, where these famous marsupials have developed more than huge number of years. From parched deserts to lavish seaside locales, kangaroos have adjusted to many conditions, displaying remarkable ways of behaving that add to their endurance and biological effect.

Regular Territory:

Topographical Conveyance:

Kangaroos are local to Australia, and their appropriation traverses the whole landmass. They are especially pervasive in open scenes, including prairies, savannas, forests, and scrublands. Various types of kangaroos have adjusted to explicit locales, bringing about a different scope of environments they call home.

Parched and Semi-Bone-dry Conditions:

Some kangaroo species, like the Red Kangaroo (Macropus rufus), flourish in parched and semi-bone-dry areas. These regions present difficulties like outrageous temperatures and restricted water sources, yet kangaroos have advanced striking variations to adapt to these cruel circumstances.

Waterfront and Forested Regions:

Different species, similar to the Eastern Dark Kangaroo (Macropus giganteus), favor seaside locales and forested regions. These natural surroundings offer an alternate arrangement of difficulties and assets, displaying the flexibility of kangaroos to different environmental specialties.

Biological system Jobs:

Kangaroos assume critical parts in molding their biological systems. As herbivores, they impact vegetation design and circulation through their taking care of propensities, making them fundamental parts of Australia's biodiversity. Their presence adds to the perplexing equilibrium of hunter prey connections and the general soundness of the environment.

Standards of conduct:

Social Design:

Kangaroos are social creatures, frequently shaping gatherings known as crowds or troops. These gatherings differ in size and arrangement, with prevailing guys, known as "boomers," driving and safeguarding the horde. Females and their posterity, known as "joeys," comprise most of the gathering.

Correspondence:

Kangaroos impart through a blend of vocalizations, non-verbal communication, and actual collaborations. Snorts, snaps, and murmuring sounds are among the vocalizations utilized for correspondence inside the horde. Non-verbal communication, including stances and developments, passes on data about friendly ordered progression and expected dangers.

Bouncing Motion:

One of the most particular elements of kangaroos is their bouncing headway. Their strong rear legs, adjusted for hopping, permit them to cover enormous distances with striking rate and proficiency. This special type of development monitors energy and is appropriate to the extensive scenes of Australia.

Touching Way of behaving:

Kangaroos are herbivores, essentially touching on an assortment of vegetation. Their eating regimen incorporates grasses, bushes, leaves, and, surprisingly, certain organic products. The specific touching way of behaving of kangaroos has biological ramifications, impacting the creation and design of vegetation in their natural surroundings.

Nighttime and Crepuscular Movement:

Kangaroos are crepuscular and nighttime, meaning they are generally dynamic during sunrise, sunset, and over the course of the evening. This conduct is accepted to be a variation to the difficult ecological states of numerous Australian areas, where daytime temperatures can be outrageous.

Conceptive Techniques:

Kangaroos show one of a kind regenerative procedures. Female kangaroos have two uteri and the capacity to defer the advancement of an incipient organism until natural circumstances are ideal. This variation guarantees the endurance of youthful kangaroos, known as joeys, who spend a huge part of their initial improvement in the security of the mother's pocket.

Horde Elements:

Inside a horde, kangaroos lay out a social progressive system. Predominant guys, recognized by their bigger size and actual ability, accept influential positions. Females and their joeys structure an intently sew social unit, offering help and insurance to each other. The social elements inside a crowd add to the general soundness of the gathering.

Transient Way of behaving:

Some kangaroo species show transitory way of behaving, getting across huge distances looking for food and water. This roaming way of life is a reaction to the erratic and variable states of the Australian scene, permitting kangaroos to adjust to changing natural elements.

Transformations to the Climate:

Thermoregulation:

Kangaroos have created proficient thermoregulation instruments to adapt to Australia's variable environment. Licking their forelimbs, known as "forelimb licking," is a way of behaving that assists them with chilling off by advancing intensity misfortune through the vanishing of spit.

Water Reliance:

While kangaroos have variations to limit water misfortune, they actually expect water to get by. They acquire a portion of their water needs from the dampness content of the vegetation they polish off. Furthermore, regular water sources like streams, lakes, and waterholes assume a critical part in their endurance, particularly in parched locales.

Hunter Aversion:

Kangaroos have developed techniques to stay away from hunters, including their particular jumping walk that takes into account quick getaway. Their sharp detects, including intense hearing and an advanced feeling of smell, assist them with identifying likely dangers. In open scenes, perceivability is a key benefit, permitting kangaroos to recognize hunters from a good ways.

Specific Taking care of:

Kangaroos are particular slow eaters, picking explicit plants in view of their wholesome substance. This specific taking care of conduct has biological ramifications, as it impacts the creation and design of vegetation in their environments. It additionally mirrors their capacity to adjust to fluctuating food accessibility in various conditions.

Collaborations with Different Species:

Concurrence with Different Herbivores:

Kangaroos share their natural surroundings with a different cluster of untamed life, including different herbivores like wallabies, wombats, and different bird species. The associations among kangaroos and different herbivores add to the perplexing trap of environmental connections inside their biological systems.

Hunters and Dangers:

Regardless of their spryness and speed, kangaroos face predation from different sources. Normal hunters incorporate dingoes, hawks, and enormous reptiles. Human-prompted dangers, like territory annihilation, vehicle crashes, and hunting, additionally present huge dangers to kangaroo populaces.

Seed Dispersal:

Kangaroos incidentally add to seed dispersal as they get across scenes. Seeds from the plants they consume can be moved in their dung, helping with the recovery of vegetation and affecting plant dispersion.

Protection Importance:

Social Significance:

Kangaroos hold social importance for Native Australian people group. They highlight unmistakably in Dreamtime stories, customary workmanship, and ceremonies. The connection between native individuals and kangaroos reaches out past fables, as these creatures have been a wellspring of food, dress, and devices for Native people group for millennia.

Preservation Status:

While kangaroos are not as of now delegated imperiled, a few animal varieties face confined dangers and populace declines because of natural surroundings misfortune, human exercises, and environmental change. Preservation endeavors center around protecting their normal territories and tending to the difficulties they experience in an undeniably human-ruled scene.

The travel industry and Instructive Worth:

Kangaroos are a significant fascination for natural life the travel industry in Australia, drawing guests from around the world. Their social importance and special ways of behaving make them a point of convergence for eco-the travel industry drives, adding to neighborhood economies and bringing issues to light about the significance of natural life protection.

1.2Importance of Kangaroos in Ecosystems

Kangaroos, with their unmistakable bouncing step and famous presence in Australia's immense scenes, assume a crucial and complex part in environments. Past their social importance and alluring allure, kangaroos are indispensable parts of the many-sided snare of life. This exhaustive investigation digs into the different elements of the significance of kangaroos in biological systems, analyzing their natural, ecological, and socio-social commitments.

1. **Biological Importance**
1. **Vegetation Guideline and Perusing Conduct**

   One of the essential biological jobs of kangaroos lies in their effect on vegetation. As herbivores, kangaroos take part in specific perusing, affecting the construction and structure of plant networks. This particular taking care of conduct forestalls the strength of explicit plant species, elevating biodiversity and adding to a fair biological system.

2. **Seed Dispersal**

   Kangaroos unintentionally go about as seed dispersers as they navigate various territories. Seeds from the plants they consume are shipped in their defecation, working with the recovery of vegetation in different regions. This cycle helps with keeping up with hereditary variety inside plant populaces and supports the versatility of environments.

3. **Biological system Specialists**

Kangaroos capability as biological system engineers, effectively forming their surroundings through their scavenging propensities. By impacting vegetation structure, kangaroos add to the production of microhabitats, giving open doors to different species to flourish. This designing job exhibits the interconnectedness of species inside biological systems.

II. Ecological Transformations

1. **Dry season Opposition and Water Preservation**

   In the bone-dry and semi-parched districts where kangaroos are pervasive, their transformations to water shortage are essential. Kangaroos can acquire a portion of their water needs from the dampness content of the vegetation they drink, limiting their reliance on outer water sources. This capacity to flourish in water-scant conditions adds to environment dependability in parched scenes.

2. Thermoregulation Methodologies

Australia's different environments open kangaroos to changing temperatures. Their proficient thermoregulation components, including forelimb licking to cool themselves, permit them to adjust to both hot and cold circumstances. This flexibility empowers kangaroos to possess many biological systems, exhibiting their versatility despite natural difficulties.

III. Biotic Connections

1. Hunter Prey Elements

Kangaroos, as herbivores, structure a basic part of the prey base in biological systems. Their cooperations with normal hunters, for example, dingoes and falcons, add to the guideline of hunter prey elements. These elements assume an essential part in keeping up with the wellbeing and equilibrium of environments, forestalling uncontrolled populace development of the two herbivores and hunters.

2. Conjunction with Other Untamed life

Kangaroos share their living spaces with a different exhibit of untamed life, including different herbivores, birds, and reptiles. The conjunction of kangaroos with different species encourages unpredictable environmental connections, making a complicated trap of collaborations. This biodiversity is fundamental for the general flexibility and versatility of biological systems.

IV. Social and Financial Significance

1. Social Importance in Native People group

Kangaroos hold significant social importance for Native Australian people group. They highlight noticeably in Dreamtime stories, conventional craftsmanship, and customs. Past social legacy, kangaroos have been a wellspring of food, dress, and devices for Native people group for centuries, underscoring their fundamental job in the social texture of Australia.

2. Untamed life The travel industry and Monetary Commitments

Kangaroos are significant attractions for untamed life the travel industry in Australia. Their presence draws guests from around the world, adding to neighborhood economies through eco-the travel industry drives. The monetary advantages got from untamed life the travel industry highlight the significance of kangaroos biologically as well as in supporting reasonable vocations.

V. Protection Difficulties and Methodologies

1. Human-Untamed life Struggle

As human populaces grow and infringe upon regular natural surroundings, clashes among kangaroos and people can emerge. Issues like vehicle impacts, harm to horticultural yields, and rivalry for assets feature the difficulties of conjunction. Creating supportable procedures to address these contentions is fundamental for the protection of kangaroo populaces.

2. Preservation Endeavors and Untamed life The executives

Protection drives center around safeguarding the normal natural surroundings of kangaroos and tending to the dangers they face. Supportable natural life the board rehearses plan to work out some kind of harmony between human necessities and the safeguarding of kangaroo populaces. Examination into populace elements, territory protection, and human-untamed life struggle moderation assumes a significant part in powerful preservation procedures.

1.3 Threats to Wild Kangaroo Populations

Wild kangaroo populaces in Australia face a heap of dangers that imperil their endurance and natural jobs. As notorious images of Australian untamed life, kangaroos assume significant parts in keeping up with biological system equilibrium and biodiversity. Be that as it may, the raising human-untamed life struggle, living space misfortune, environmental change, and illness episodes present critical difficulties to the supportability of kangaroo populaces. This exhaustive investigation investigates the diverse dangers going up against wild kangaroo populaces and looks at the mind boggling interchange between natural, ecological, and anthropogenic elements.

II. Environment Misfortune and Fracture

1. Urbanization and Framework Improvement

The persistent development of metropolitan regions and foundation projects is a significant driver of natural surroundings misfortune for kangaroo populaces. Expanding human settlements infringe upon customary kangaroo territories, dividing scenes and restricting the accessible space for these marsupials to openly wander. This territory misfortune disturbs relocation designs, taking care of grounds, and social designs, prompting populace decline and expanded weakness to different dangers.

2. Horticultural Development

Horticultural exercises, including animals brushing and yield development, add to natural surroundings discontinuity and debasement. Kangaroos, seeking assets with tamed creatures, frequently face food shortage and decreased admittance to water sources. The change of normal scenes into rural regions lessens appropriate environments as well as escalates human-natural life struggle as kangaroos rummage on developed crops.

III. Human-Natural life Struggle

1. Crop Harm and Domesticated animals Contest

As kangaroo environments recoil because of urbanization and horticulture, kangaroos progressively adventure into developed fields, making harm crops. Ranchers, trying to safeguard their livelihoods, may turn to separating or deadly control measures. Moreover, rivalry for brushing regions with homegrown animals can prompt contentions, worsening the difficulties looked by kangaroo populaces.

2. Vehicle Impacts

The infringement of metropolitan regions into normal living spaces carries kangaroos into closeness to streets. Vehicle impacts represent a huge danger to kangaroos, bringing about wounds and fatalities. The ascent in street organizations, particularly in districts where kangaroos are bountiful, escalates the gamble of crashes, affecting both kangaroo populaces and street wellbeing.

IV. Environmental Change and Ecological Stressors

1. Outrageous Climate Occasions

Environmental change achieves an expansion in the recurrence and force of outrageous climate occasions, including dry spells, fierce blazes, and heatwaves. These occasions present direct dangers to kangaroo populaces by causing water shortage, diminishing food accessibility, and prompting territory obliteration. The resultant ecological stressors compromise the wellbeing and conceptive progress of kangaroos, adding to populace decline.

2. Changed Vegetation Examples

Environmental change can prompt changes in vegetation designs, affecting the accessibility and nature of food hotspots for kangaroos. Changes in plant sythesis and appropriation might disturb the fragile harmony among herbivores and their living spaces, influencing kangaroo sustenance and generally prosperity. Variation to these adjusted environments presents difficulties that can additionally pressure wild kangaroo populaces.

V. Illness Episodes and Biosecurity Concerns

1. Arising Irresistible Illnesses

Illness flare-ups, especially those brought about by arising irresistible specialists, represent a serious danger to wild kangaroo populaces. Infections, microorganisms, and parasites sent between kangaroos or from different species can bring about populace declines and compromise individual wellbeing. Factors, for example, environmental change and living space interruption can add to the development and spread of irresistible illnesses among kangaroo populaces.

2. **Biosecurity Dangers from Homegrown Creatures**

The collaboration between wild kangaroos and homegrown creatures presents biosecurity gambles. Homegrown animals can send sicknesses to kangaroos, influencing their wellbeing and regenerative achievement. Keeping a fragile harmony between the soundness of homegrown creatures and the protection of wild kangaroo populaces is pivotal for forestalling illness episodes.

VI. Hunting and Poaching

1. **Business and Sporting Hunting**
   Kangaroos are exposed to both business and sporting hunting, with the cowhide and meat enterprises driving interest for kangaroo items. The controlled winnowing of kangaroos has financial ramifications however raises moral worries and requires cautious administration to guarantee manageability. Unregulated and unlawful hunting, driven by underground market requests, compounds the strain on kangaroo populaces and undermines their drawn out endurance.

2. **Creature Government assistance Concerns**

The techniques utilized in business kangaroo hunting have started discusses with respect to creature government assistance. Concerns incorporate the treatment of harmed or stranded joeys, the exactness of shooting rehearses, and the effect of hunting exercises on friendly designs inside kangaroo populaces. Finding some kind of harmony between preservation endeavors, financial contemplations, and moral treatment is fundamental for tending to the dangers presented by hunting.

VII. Preservation Difficulties and The board Systems

1. **Populace Checking and Exploration**
   Viable preservation the executives starts with thorough populace observing and research drives. Understanding kangaroo socioeconomics, relocation designs, and hereditary variety gives an establishment to confirm based preservation techniques. Ceaseless observing takes into account opportune mediations and versatile administration practices to address arising dangers.

2. **Environment Insurance and Rebuilding**
   Safeguarding and reestablishing normal natural surroundings are basic parts of kangaroo protection. Executing measures to shield crucial territories from additional corruption, alongside territory rebuilding projects, guarantees the

accessibility of reasonable conditions for kangaroo populaces to flourish. Availability between environments works with normal ways of behaving, relocation, and hereditary trade.

3. **Local area Commitment and Instruction**

   Drawing in neighborhood networks in preservation endeavors cultivates a feeling of shared liability. Instructive projects that feature the natural significance of kangaroos, advance concurrence systems, and address human-untamed life clashes are essential. Building mindfulness about the worth of kangaroos inside environments supports reasonable practices and diminishes the adverse consequence of human exercises.

4. **Natural life Passages and Network**

   Making natural life passages and keeping up with network between divided territories are fundamental for working with the development of kangaroo populaces. These passageways take into consideration normal ways of behaving like movement, scrounging, and reproducing, advancing hereditary variety and adding to the drawn out reasonability of kangaroo populaces.

5. **Strategy Advancement and Guideline**

   Strong administrative structures are fundamental for overseeing human-natural life struggle, hunting practices, and land use. Executing approaches that balance monetary interests, preservation objectives, and moral contemplations is principal. Ordinary evaluations and acclimations to these approaches guarantee their pertinence despite evolving natural, social, and financial circumstances.

6. **Environmental Change Moderation and Transformation**

   Tending to the effects of environmental change on kangaroo territories requires both relief and variation techniques. Endeavors to lessen ozone harming substance outflows add to worldwide environmental change alleviation.
   Simultaneously, versatile measures, for example, living space rebuilding, water source the executives, and practical land use arranging, assist kangaroo populaces with adapting to the evolving environment.

7. **Biosecurity Measures**

   Carrying out biosecurity measures is fundamental for forestalling illness episodes in wild kangaroo populaces. Observing the wellbeing of both homegrown and wild creatures, carrying out infectious prevention conventions, and limiting the gamble of illness transmission through successful quarantine measures add to biosecurity endeavors.

8. **Moral and Feasible Hunting Practices**

Controlling hunting practices to guarantee moral treatment, altruistic killing techniques, and reasonable collecting is vital for offsetting monetary interests with preservation objectives. Cooperation between traditionalists, trackers, and policymakers can bring about rules that focus on both the government assistance of kangaroo populaces and the monetary advantages got from directed hunting.

Chapter 2

Captive Environments: Past And Present

The set of experiences and development of hostage conditions for creatures have been set apart by a mind boggling transaction of human inspirations, logical headways, moral contemplations, and changing cultural perspectives towards natural life. This extensive investigation digs into the over a wide span of time of hostage conditions, following the improvement of zoos, aquariums, and different offices intended to house and exhibit different species. The account will look at the verifiable setting of bondage, the development of nook configuration, altering points of view on creature government assistance, and contemporary practices pointed toward giving improving and reasonable conditions.

II. Early Acts of Bondage

1. **Zoos and Regal Assortments**
   The idea of saving colorful creatures for show traces all the way back to antiquated civic establishments, where rulers and honorability frequently kept up with zoological displays as images of riches and influence. These early types of bondage were described by an emphasis on extraordinariness and exoticism, with little thought for the government assistance and normal ways of behaving of the creatures.

2. **Carnivals and Voyaging Shows**

In the nineteenth and mid twentieth hundreds of years, bazaars and voyaging shows became noticeable scenes for displaying outlandish creatures. While giving diversion to the majority, these conditions were set apart by little and frequently insufficient nooks, restricted veterinary consideration, and an emphasis on exhibition instead of creature prosperity.

III. Advancement of Hostage Conditions

1. **The Rise of Present day Zoos**
   The late nineteenth century saw the foundation of current zoos with a shift towards a more protection situated approach. Zoos started to zero in on schooling, research, and the conservation of imperiled species. Striking establishments, for example, the London Zoo and the Bronx Zoo, assumed urgent parts in changing the impression of imprisonment from simple display to focuses of preservation and schooling.
2. **Aquariums and Marine Parks**

Lined up with the improvement of zoos, aquariums and marine parks arose to exhibit sea-going life. Establishments like SeaWorld presented creative showcases that permitted guests to observe marine creatures in settings looking like their normal territories. Be that as it may, the imprisonment of marine vertebrates in these offices has ignited moral discussions and prompted expanded examination throughout the long term.

IV. Having an impact on Viewpoints on Creature Government assistance

1. **Shift Towards Moral Contemplations**
   As' how society might interpret creature cognizance and government assistance developed, there was a change in perspective in the objectives and practices of hostage conditions. Moral contemplations started to assume a more huge part, inciting a reassessment of nook plan, veterinary consideration, and the mental prosperity of hostage creatures.
2. **The Job of License and Norms**

The foundation of certifying bodies, like the Relationship of Zoos and Aquariums (AZA) and the World Relationship of Zoos and Aquariums (WAZA), achieved normalized rules for creature care and the executives. Certification processes became essential to keeping up with elevated requirements in hostage offices, guaranteeing an emphasis on protection, training, and moral treatment of creatures.

V. Progresses in Fenced in area Plan and Creature Government assistance

1. **Social Advancement and Naturalistic Territories**
   Current hostage conditions focus on conduct enhancement and the formation of naturalistic territories. Enhancement exercises emulate creatures' regular ways of behaving, advancing physical and mental excitement. Nooks are intended to repeat the creatures' local surroundings, encouraging a feeling that everything is good and considering more regular ways of behaving.
2. **Innovation Incorporation**

Progressions in innovation have altered how hostage conditions are made due. CCTV cameras, temperature control frameworks, and remote observing apparatuses empower staff to screen creature conduct, wellbeing, and prosperity. This joining of innovation upgrades both creature care and the instructive experience for guests.

VI. Protection and Instructive Jobs

1. Protection Reproducing Projects

Numerous cutting edge zoos and hostage offices effectively take part in preservation reproducing programs. These drives center around rearing imperiled species in imprisonment with a definitive objective of once again introducing them into their regular natural surroundings. The progress of projects like the California Condor recuperation exertion features the possible effect of hostage conditions on worldwide biodiversity.

2. Training and Public Mindfulness

Hostage conditions play progressively embraced their part as instructive foundations. Zoos and aquariums give guests chances to find out about biodiversity, biological systems, and the significance of preservation. Instructive projects, intelligent displays, and directed visits add to raising public mindfulness and encouraging a feeling of obligation towards untamed life preservation.

VII. Moral Difficulties and Debates

1. Basic entitlements and Backing

The moral quandaries encompassing hostage conditions have led to basic entitlements developments and backing gatherings. Activists contend against the imprisonment of wild creatures, refering to worries about restricted space, unnatural ways of behaving, and the mental prosperity of hostage people. The discussion over the morals of imprisonment keeps on forming popular assessment and impact the approaches of hostage offices.

2. Debates in Marine Parks

Marine parks, specifically, have confronted elevated examination and public reaction because of contentions encompassing the treatment of marine warm blooded animals in bondage. Narratives like "Blackfish" pointed out the difficulties looked by orcas in bondage, prompting expanded requires the finish of hostage reproducing and public exhibitions including marine well evolved creatures.

VIII. Future Bearings and Advancements

1. Headways in Veterinary Consideration

Progressing examination and headways in veterinary consideration add to the prosperity of creatures in bondage. Particular clinical consideration, dietary projects, and preventive medical care measures guarantee that creatures in hostage conditions get the consideration expected to keep up with their wellbeing.

2. **Computer generated Reality and Increased Reality Encounters**
   Because of worries about creature government assistance and preservation, a few offices are investigating computer generated reality (VR) and increased reality (AR) encounters as options in contrast to customary hostage conditions. These innovations offer vivid and instructive encounters without the actual presence of hostage creatures, tending to a few moral worries related with conventional displays.

3. **Cooperative Protection Drives**

The fate of hostage conditions lies in cooperative endeavors between establishments, preservation associations, and neighborhood networks. Cooperative preservation drives center around saving regular environments, supporting neighborhood networks, and incorporating logical exploration to upgrade the general effect of hostage offices on worldwide biodiversity.

2.1 Historical Perspectives on Captive Kangaroos

Hostage kangaroos have a celebrated history that mirrors the developing connection among people and untamed life. From the beginning of European investigation in Australia to the present, the bondage of kangaroos has gone through huge movements, driven by variables like interest, exhibitionism, logical request, and preservation endeavors. This exhaustive investigation digs into the authentic viewpoints on hostage kangaroos, following their excursion from inquisitive oddities to envoys for preservation and instruction.

II. Early Experiences and Interests

1. **European Investigation and Interest**
   The primary recorded experiences among Europeans and kangaroos happened during the Time of Investigation in the late eighteenth hundred years. These surprising marsupials entranced travelers and naturalists, inciting some to catch live examples for study and display. Kangaroos became inquisitive curiosities, highlighted in zoos and confidential assortments across Europe.

2. **Display in Zoological gardens and Zoos**

As European powers laid out provinces in Australia, the interest with Australian fauna heightened. Kangaroos were shipped off Europe and North America to be shown in zoological displays and zoos. These early hostage conditions were portrayed by restricted information on kangaroo science and government assistance, prompting difficulties in giving reasonable consideration to these novel marsupials.

III. Logical Investigation and Study

1. **Ordered Arrangement and Investigation of Conduct**
   Logical interest in kangaroos developed as naturalists looked to grasp their scientific categorization, conduct, and biological jobs. Hostage conditions gave chances to close perception and study. Early endeavors to group different kangaroo species and report their ways of behaving added to the more extensive comprehension of Australian marsupials.
2. **Commitments to Transformative Science**

Kangaroos, as extraordinary delegates of marsupials, assumed a part in conversations about developmental science. The investigation of their life systems, regenerative techniques, and variations gave significant bits of knowledge into the more extensive setting of mammalian advancement. Hostage examples became subjects of logical investigation, revealing insight into the variety of life on The planet.

IV. Exhibitionism and Diversion

1. **Bazaars and Voyaging Shows**
   In the nineteenth and mid twentieth hundreds of years, kangaroos tracked down their direction into bazaars and voyaging shows, turning out to be essential for media outlets. The traveling way of life of these shows frequently prompted testing conditions for hostage kangaroos, as they were exposed to visit transport, little walled in areas, and the tensions of performing for crowds.
2. **Colorful Attractions in Pilgrim Presentations**

Frontier presentations, normal in the late nineteenth and mid twentieth hundreds of years, displayed the riches and variety of supreme powers. Kangaroos, close by other Australian untamed life, were displayed as intriguing attractions, supporting pilgrim stories and adding to the view of Australia as a far off and secretive land.

V. Moving Points of view and Moral Contemplations

1. **Development of Zoo Theory**
   The mid-twentieth century denoted a change in zoo reasoning, creating some distance from simply grandstander practices to embrace protection, training, and moral contemplations. Zoos started to focus on the prosperity of creatures in imprisonment, accentuating naturalistic walled in areas, advancement exercises, and rearing projects to help imperiled species.
2. **Protection and Rearing Projects**

As familiarity with untamed life preservation developed, kangaroos took on another job in hostage conditions. Zoos and natural life stops effectively partook in reproducing programs pointed toward saving hereditary variety and forestalling the decay of specific kangaroo species. Hostage conditions became center points for exploration and preservation endeavors.

VI. Instructive Drives and Public Mindfulness

1. Job of Hostage Kangaroos in Schooling

Hostage kangaroos progressed from simple interests to instructive envoys. Zoos and untamed life parks utilized the presence of kangaroos to teach people in general about Australian environments, biodiversity, and the significance of preservation. Instructive drives intended to impart a feeling of obligation and stewardship among guests.

2. Intuitive Displays and Preservation Informing

Present day hostage conditions embraced intelligent displays to connect with guests in a more vivid instructive experience. Protection informing stressed the difficulties looked by kangaroos in the wild, including living space misfortune, environmental change, and human-natural life struggle. Hostage kangaroos became images of more extensive protection issues.

VII. Difficulties and Discussions

1. Moral Worries in Hostage Conditions

Regardless of progressions in the moral treatment of hostage creatures, challenges continue. Pundits contend that even the most very much planned walled in areas can't completely reproduce the mind boggling regular ways of behaving of kangaroos in nature. Moral worries likewise reach out to issues like space impediments, social elements, and the mental prosperity of hostage people.

2. Public Discussions on Bondage

Public discussions in regards to the morals of keeping kangaroos in imprisonment keep on molding the approaches of zoos and natural life parks. Basic entitlements advocates question the need of hostage conditions, requiring a reexamination of the job of zoos in protection and schooling. These discussions brief continuous reflection on the moral ramifications of bondage.

VIII. Future Headings and Preservation Difficulties

1. Developments in Hostage Conditions

The eventual fate of hostage kangaroos might include creative ways to deal with address moral worries. Propels in fenced in area plan, conduct improvement, and innovation coordination mean to upgrade the prosperity of hostage people. Computer generated reality encounters might offer options in contrast to customary shows, giving instructive open doors without actual imprisonment.

2. Protection Difficulties in Nature

As the difficulties confronting kangaroos in the wild heighten, the job of hostage conditions in protection turns out to be more basic. Living space misfortune, environmental change, and human-untamed life struggle present critical dangers to kangaroo populaces. Hostage reproducing projects and examination drives mean to add to the preservation of these notorious marsupials.

2.2 Evolution of Captive Enclosures

The development of hostage nooks is a demonstration of the having a significant impact on points of view on creature government assistance, protection, and training. From the beginning of zoological displays with simple enclosures to the refined shows in present day zoos and untamed life stops, the plan and reasoning behind hostage walled in areas have gone through huge changes. This investigation dives into the verifiable and contemporary development of hostage nooks, inspecting the variables that have impacted their turn of events and the continuous endeavors to figure out some kind of harmony between the prosperity of hostage creatures, preservation objectives, and instructive targets.

II. Early Zoological displays and Interest Cupboards

1. **Zoological displays of Ancient history**

   The idea of saving outlandish creatures for show traces all the way back to old civilizations, where rulers and respectability kept up with zoological gardens as images of force and esteem. Early zoological gardens included straightforward nooks that gave restricted space and conveniences to the hostage creatures. The essential spotlight was on exhibiting the unique case and exoticism of the animals.

2. **Interest Cupboards in the Renaissance**

During the Renaissance, the assortment and show of colorful examples in "cupboards of interests" became trendy among European privileged. Creatures were many times housed in little enclosures or compartments, underscoring their uniqueness as opposed to accommodating their prosperity. These early types of bondage were driven by interest and a craving to exhibit the marvels of the normal world.

III. Progress to Current Zoos

1. **Change in Way of thinking**

   The nineteenth century denoted a critical change in the way of thinking behind hostage conditions. The rise of present day zoos was portrayed by a change from an emphasis on simple exhibitionism to contemplations of creature government assistance, logical review, and preservation. Zoos became organizations with a mission to teach the general population, add to logical information, and effectively partake in preservation endeavors.

2. **Early Zoo Nooks**

The early fenced in areas in current zoos frequently mirrored the restricted comprehension of creature conduct and government assistance at that point. Creatures were housed in concrete or iron-banned fenced in areas that expected to give perceivability to guests yet needed thought for the regular requirements and ways of behaving of the occupants. Creatures were frequently seen as displays as opposed to conscious creatures.

IV. Ethological Experiences and Social Improvement

1. **Impact of Ethology**
    The mid-twentieth century saw the development of ethology as a logical discipline concentrating on creature conduct. Ethological bits of knowledge featured the significance of giving hostage creatures conditions that took into account normal ways of behaving and mental excitement. This change in understanding provoked a reexamination of nook plan and the executives rehearses.
2. **Presentation of Conduct Advancement**

Conduct enhancement turned into a critical idea in hostage creature the executives. Fenced in areas were overhauled to incorporate elements that supported normal ways of behaving, like climbing structures, concealing spots, and open doors for searching. The objective was to improve the physical and mental prosperity of hostage creatures, diminishing pressure and advancing a more normal way of life.

V. Naturalistic Plan and Scene Inundation

1. **Naturalistic Nooks**
    Headways in understanding creature conduct and government assistance prompted the advancement of naturalistic fenced in areas. These nooks mean to recreate the creatures' regular territories, giving a more vivid and true insight for both the occupants and the guests. Naturalistic elements incorporate vegetation, water includes, and fluctuated territory, permitting creatures to communicate a more extensive scope of ways of behaving.
2. **Scene Inundation**

The idea of scene submersion takes naturalistic plan to a higher level. Rather than isolating creatures from guests with obstructions, scene drenching permits guests to see creatures in conditions that intently look like their local natural surroundings. This approach cultivates a feeling of association among guests and the normal ways of behaving of the creatures, advancing compassion and understanding.

VI. Preservation centered Nooks

1. **Preservation Rearing Projects**
    As zoos and natural life parks embraced a protection mission, hostage nooks

became necessary to rearing projects for jeopardized species. Nooks were intended to help rearing ways of behaving, propagation, and the raising of posterity. The objective was not exclusively to keep up with hereditary variety yet additionally to add to the populace recuperation of undermined species.

2. **Walled in areas as Protection Features**

Current hostage nooks act as features for protection drives. Interpretive signage, intelligent shows, and in the background visits teach guests about the difficulties looked by species in the wild and the job of hostage conditions in protection. Nooks become stages for bringing issues to light and encouraging a feeling of obligation toward worldwide biodiversity.

VII. Innovative Joining

1. **Reconnaissance and Observing**
   Headways in innovation have reformed the administration of hostage walled in areas. Reconnaissance cameras, sensors, and checking frameworks permit overseers to notice creature conduct, track wellbeing measurements, and guarantee the security of the two creatures and guests. This innovative coordination upgrades the effectiveness of hostage creature care.

2. **Computer generated Reality Encounters**

With an end goal to address moral worries related with imprisonment, a few offices investigate computer generated reality (VR) encounters as options in contrast to conventional nooks. VR advances offer guests vivid experiences with creatures and their natural surroundings without the actual requirements of imprisonment. This approach means to give instructive open doors while limiting the effect on the prosperity of hostage creatures.

VIII. Challenges and Moral Contemplations

1. **Space Constraints and Social Limitations**
   Indeed, even with headways in nook configuration, space constraints stay a test in hostage conditions. A few creatures, especially those with broad home reaches in the wild, may encounter conduct limitations in imprisonment. Moral worries emerge when fenced in areas can't sufficiently oblige the regular ways of behaving and needs of the occupants.

2. **Social Elements and Gathering Living**

Fenced in areas intended for social species should consider the intricacies of gathering living. Social elements, order, and similarity among people become urgent variables in nook plan. At times, challenges emerge while endeavoring to recreate normal social designs inside the bounds of imprisonment.

IX. Future Headings and Imaginative Plans

1. **Supportable and Eco-accommodating Walled in areas**

   The eventual fate of hostage walled in areas is probably going to underline maintainability and eco-amicability. Green plan standards, sustainable power sources, and territory reclamation inside hostage conditions mean to lessen the natural impression of these offices. Nooks might incorporate flawlessly with encompassing biological systems, adding to more extensive protection objectives.

2. **Public Commitment through Intuitive Plan**

Proceeded with advancement in walled in area configuration will zero in on improving public commitment. Intelligent shows, computer generated reality encounters, and instructive projects will assume a focal part in interfacing guests with the normal world. Nooks will become vivid learning conditions that encourage a more profound comprehension of natural life and preservation.

2.3 Current Practices and Trends in Kangaroo Captivity

The bondage of kangaroos has gone through critical changes as of late, reflecting advancing perspectives towards creature government assistance, preservation, and schooling. As notorious images of Australia's extraordinary natural life, kangaroos hold a unique spot in the hearts of the two local people and guests. This complete investigation digs into the ongoing practices and patterns in kangaroo bondage, looking at the difficulties looked by these marsupials, the endeavors to upgrade their prosperity in hostage conditions, and the job of such settings in adding to preservation and government funded schooling.

II. Hostage Conditions: Types and Qualities

1. **Zoos and Untamed life Parks**

   Zoos and natural life parks keep on being essential settings for hostage kangaroos. These offices differ in size, going from little nearby zoos to huge, universally perceived natural life asylums. Nooks are intended to give naturalistic conditions, consolidating highlights like open spaces, vegetation, and taking care of regions that impersonate the kangaroos' local territories.

2. **Asylums and Salvages**

Safe-havens and salvage focuses assume a urgent part being taken care of by harmed, stranded, or dislodged kangaroos. These offices focus on restoration and delivery, intending to return restored people to the wild whenever the situation allows. Fenced in areas in asylums frequently center around establishing conditions that help the kangaroos' physical and emotional well-being during their visit.

III. Moral Contemplations and Creature Government assistance

1. Space and Walled in area Plan

Moral contemplations in kangaroo imprisonment base on giving adequate room and proper walled in area plan. Bigger nooks that take into consideration jumping, brushing, and social collaborations are viewed as fundamental for the prosperity of kangaroos. Naturalistic highlights, like shakes and trees, give open doors to social improvement.

2. Social Elements and Gathering Living

Kangaroos are social creatures that flourish in social environments. Current practices focus on the comprehension of social elements inside kangaroo gatherings. Nooks are intended to work with regular social associations, and guardians screen collective vibes to guarantee similarity and limit pressure.

3. Conduct Advancement

Conduct enhancement assumes a vital part in improving the prosperity of hostage kangaroos. Enhancement exercises, like riddle feeders, searching open doors, and climbing structures, are integrated into everyday schedules. These exercises animate regular ways of behaving, forestall fatigue, and add to the psychological and actual strength of the kangaroos.

IV. Protection and Reproducing Projects

1. Protection Drives

Hostage kangaroo populaces add to protection drives, especially for imperiled or weak species. A few offices participate in reproducing programs pointed toward keeping up with hereditary variety and making hold populaces. These projects act as a type of protection against populace decreases in nature.

2. Delivery and Renewed introduction Endeavors

Safe-havens and protect focuses effectively take part in delivery and renewed introduction programs. Kangaroos that have gone through recovery and are considered fit for endurance in the wild are delivered into reasonable environments. Observing and post-discharge support are indispensable parts of these endeavors.

V. Challenges in Kangaroo Bondage

1. Illness The board

Illness the board is a critical test in hostage kangaroo conditions. Closeness inside walled in areas builds the gamble of sickness transmission. Offices carry out thorough wellbeing checking programs, quarantine measures, and inoculation conventions to relieve the spread of irresistible sicknesses.

2. Human-Untamed life Struggle

Human-untamed life struggle is a worry, particularly in regions where kangaroos come into close contact with human populaces. Offices close to metropolitan regions might confront difficulties, for example, vehicle crashes, crop harm, and clashes with homegrown creatures. Methodologies for dealing with these struggles incorporate the production of natural life hallways and public mindfulness crusades.

VI. Government funded Training and Mindfulness

1. Interpretive Projects

Hostage kangaroo conditions act as instructive stages to raise public mindfulness about these notorious marsupials and the protection challenges they face. Interpretive projects, directed visits, and intuitive shows furnish guests with data about kangaroo science, conduct, and the significance of safeguarding their normal natural surroundings.

2. Virtual Commitment

Because of worries about the effect of guest connections on creature government assistance, a few offices investigate virtual commitment choices. Computer generated reality encounters, live-streaming cameras, and online instructive assets permit individuals to interface with kangaroos without truly visiting an office.

These drives extend the span of instructive projects while limiting unsettling influences to the creatures.

VII. Feasible Practices and Eco-accommodating Walled in areas

1. Practical Plan

Present day kangaroo walled in areas progressively consolidate feasible plan standards. These practices might incorporate energy-proficient lighting, water reusing frameworks, and the utilization of eco-accommodating structure materials. Maintainable plan intends to diminish the natural effect of hostage conditions and line up with more extensive preservation objectives.

2. Environment Incorporation

A few offices investigate living space incorporation, where hostage nooks consistently mix with the encompassing scene. This approach permits kangaroos to encounter conditions that intently look like their regular natural surroundings. Natural surroundings reconciliation upgrades the mental prosperity of the creatures and gives guests a more genuine encounter.

VIII. Innovative Advances

1. Observing and Exploration

Mechanical advances assume a urgent part in the observing and research endeavors inside hostage kangaroo conditions. CCTV cameras, GPS beacons, and wellbeing observing frameworks empower overseers and specialists to accumulate important information on kangaroo conduct, development examples, and generally speaking prosperity.

2. **Information driven Administration**

Information driven administration rehearses influence innovation to illuminate dynamic cycles. The assortment and examination of information on individual kangaroo wellbeing, generation, and conduct add to custom-made administration methodologies. This approach upgrades the viability of hostage care and protection endeavors.

IX. Moral The travel industry and Capable Natural life Survey

1. **Moral The travel industry Practices**
   Offices that house kangaroos are progressively taking on moral the travel industry rehearses. These practices focus on the prosperity of the creatures, accentuating capable connections with guests. Training about moral untamed life seeing, regarding limits, and limiting aggravations is essential to these drives.
2. **Guest Commitment in Protection**

Offices support guest commitment in protection endeavors. Programs that permit guests to add to protection drives, for example, territory rebuilding projects or emblematic receptions, cultivate a feeling of obligation and association with the prosperity of kangaroos in nature.

X. Future Headings and Progressing Exploration

1. **Propels in Veterinary Consideration**
   Proceeded with exploration and advances in veterinary consideration add to the prosperity of hostage kangaroos. Particular clinical consideration, wholesome projects, and preventive medical services measures guarantee that creatures in hostage conditions get the consideration expected to keep up with their wellbeing.
2. **Joint effort in Protection**

The fate of kangaroo bondage lies in cooperative preservation drives. Joint effort between foundations, protection associations, and neighborhood networks is fundamental for tending to more extensive preservation challenges, including environment misfortune, environmental change, and human-untamed life struggle.

Chapter 3

Challenges In Captive Kangaroo Management

Hostage kangaroo the executives presents a horde of difficulties that request a fragile harmony between the prosperity of the marsupials, protection objectives, and the instructive mission of the offices. As notable images of Australia's special untamed life, kangaroos in imprisonment face particular difficulties that require smart and informed administration methodologies. This far reaching investigation dives into the complex difficulties in hostage kangaroo the executives, resolving issues connected with creature government assistance, wellbeing, preservation, and the moral contemplations encompassing their bondage.

II. Moral Contemplations and Creature Government assistance

1. **Space Limits**
   One of the essential difficulties in hostage kangaroo the board is giving satisfactory room to reflect their regular ways of behaving. Kangaroos are dynamic, jumping creatures with enormous home reaches in nature. Hostage conditions, in any event, when planned with the best expectations, frequently battle to match the immensity of their normal environments.

2. **Social Elements and Gathering Living**
   Kangaroos are exceptionally friendly creatures with complex social designs. Keeping up with regular collective vibes in bondage can be testing, particularly while considering elements like similarity, order, and regional ways of behaving. Lopsided characteristics in friendly designs can prompt pressure and social issues among hostage kangaroos.

3. **Social Enhancement**

Hostage kangaroos require significant feeling to communicate their normal ways of behaving. Social advancement is critical for their physical and mental prosperity. In any case, planning compelling enhancement exercises that mirror normal ways of behaving and forestall weariness represents a consistent test for overseers.

III. Wellbeing The executives and Sickness Anticipation

1. Illness Transmission in Encased Spaces
Hostage conditions, where kangaroos frequently live in closeness, present a higher gamble of illness transmission. The spread of irresistible infections represents a huge danger to the wellbeing of hostage kangaroo populaces. Forestalling and overseeing sicknesses in encased spaces require thorough checking and veterinary mediations.

2. Stress-related Medical problems
Stress is an unavoidable worry in hostage kangaroo the board. Factors like guest collaborations, transport, and changes in friendly elements can add to pressure related medical problems. Ongoing pressure compromises the resistant framework, making kangaroos more powerless to illnesses and other medical conditions.

3. Conceptive Wellbeing Difficulties

Keeping up with conceptive wellbeing is basic for hostage kangaroo populaces, particularly for those associated with reproducing programs. Nonetheless, issues, for example, rearing troubles, low richness rates, and regenerative infections can introduce difficulties. Extensive conceptive administration procedures are fundamental to guarantee the progress of hostage rearing drives.

IV. Protection Difficulties

1. Hereditary Variety
Hostage rearing projects mean to add to the protection of kangaroo species. In any case, keeping up with hereditary variety inside hostage populaces is a consistent test. Restricted genetic supplies in bondage can bring about inbreeding, prompting hereditary issues and decreased wellness in posterity.

2. Coordination with Protection Objectives
Hostage kangaroo the executives is frequently entwined with more extensive preservation objectives. Guaranteeing that hostage conditions contribute seriously to the safeguarding of wild populaces requires cautious preparation, exploration, and joint effort between hostage offices and preservation associations.

3. Renewed introduction Situations

For safe-havens and salvage focuses associated with the restoration and arrival of kangaroos, the course of renewed introduction into the wild represents its own arrangement of difficulties. Beating potential human-natural life struggle, guaranteeing abilities to survive in restored kangaroos, and checking their prosperity post-discharge are mind boggling errands.

V. Human-Natural life Struggle in Metropolitan Conditions

1. **Vehicle Crashes**
   Kangaroos in imprisonment close to metropolitan regions face the gamble of vehicle impacts while wandering into human-ruled spaces. Making natural life passageways and carrying out traffic the board methodologies are fundamental to relieve the perils presented by streets and vehicles.
2. **Crop Harm**

In regions where kangaroos cross-over with agrarian grounds, clashes emerge because of harvest harm. Finding supportable arrangements that balance the necessities of ranchers and the protection of kangaroos is a continuous test in hostage kangaroo the board.

VI. Moral The travel industry and Guest Communications

1. **Influence on Creature Government assistance**
   The communication among guests and hostage kangaroos is a blade that cuts both ways. While it gives an open door to government funded instruction and mindfulness, it likewise presents dangers to the prosperity of the kangaroos. Excessively excited guests might pressure the creatures, and close communications might prompt the transmission of infections.
2. **Adjusting Protection Instruction and Creature Government assistance**

Instructive projects focused on guests should work out some kind of harmony between bringing issues to light about kangaroos and guaranteeing the government assistance of the hostage people. Moral the travel industry rehearses, mindful untamed life survey, and clear rules for guest cooperations are pivotal parts of this difficult exercise.

VII. Manageable Practices and Natural Effect

1. **Energy Utilization and Waste Administration**
   The natural effect of hostage kangaroo the board incorporates contemplations of energy utilization and waste administration. Feasible practices, like energy-proficient foundation and waste decrease drives, are fundamental for limiting the biological impression of hostage conditions.
2. **Living space Reconciliation and Natural Concordance**

Endeavors to incorporate hostage conditions with normal territories, known as environment mix, expect to make spaces that blend with the encompassing biological system. Accomplishing this incorporation requires smart intending to guarantee that hostage conditions contribute decidedly to neighborhood environment.

VIII. Mechanical Advances in Checking and Exploration

1. **Remote Observing and Information Assortment**
   Mechanical advances assume a vital part in tending to difficulties in kangaroo the board. Remote observing apparatuses, for example, GPS following and camera frameworks, give significant bits of knowledge into the way of behaving, wellbeing, and development examples of hostage kangaroos. These advancements work with information driven independent direction and upgrade the general administration of kangaroo populaces.
2. **Veterinary Consideration Advancements**

Headways in veterinary consideration add to the prosperity of hostage kangaroos. Specific clinical consideration, symptomatic apparatuses, and treatment choices empower overseers to address medical problems speedily. Progressing research in veterinary medication upgrades the comprehension of kangaroo physiology and pathology.

IX. Cooperative Preservation Drives

1. **Local area Commitment and Joint effort**
   Compelling kangaroo the board requires coordinated effort between hostage offices, protection associations, neighborhood networks, and legislative bodies. Local area commitment drives, cooperative examination projects, and shared preservation objectives encourage a feeling of aggregate liability regarding the government assistance and protection of kangaroos.
2. **Global Collaboration**

Some kangaroo species are disseminated across worldwide lines, underlining the requirement for global participation in protection endeavors. Cooperative drives including numerous nations plan to address transboundary preservation challenges and guarantee the assurance of kangaroos in their regular natural surroundings.

X. Future Headings and Continuous Exploration

1. **Developments in Hostage Conditions**
   The eventual fate of hostage kangaroo the executives lies in consistent advancement. Propels in nook plan, conduct enhancement, and innovation coordination will assume a vital part in tending to existing difficulties. Reasonable and eco-accommodating practices will probably turn out to be more predominant in hostage conditions.
2. **Preservation Exploration and Schooling**

Continuous examination into kangaroo conduct, biology, and wellbeing will illuminate further developed administration techniques. Preservation schooling drives will keep on developing, using innovation and creative ways to deal with draw in the general population and cultivate a more profound comprehension of the difficulties looked by kangaroos in imprisonment and nature.

3.1 Health and Welfare Issues

Guaranteeing the wellbeing and government assistance of kangaroos in hostage conditions is a complicated undertaking that requires a careful comprehension of their normal ways of behaving, physiological necessities, and the difficulties presented by imprisonment. This extensive investigation dives into the diverse issues encompassing the wellbeing and government assistance of kangaroos in bondage. From moral contemplations and conduct advancement to sickness the executives and veterinary consideration, this examination plans to reveal insight into the difficulties and likely arrangements in advancing the prosperity of these notorious marsupials.

II. Moral Contemplations and Conduct Government assistance

1. **Space Restrictions and Normal Ways of behaving**

   One of the essential moral contemplations in hostage kangaroo the executives is the arrangement of satisfactory room to consider the statement of regular ways of behaving. Kangaroos are prestigious for their jumping headway and social communications in nature. Hostage conditions should be intended to oblige these ways of behaving, forestalling the advancement of stress-related issues related with bound spaces.

2. **Social Elements and Gathering Living**

   Kangaroos are intrinsically friendly creatures with complex gathering structures. Hostage conditions frequently battle to duplicate the unpredictable social elements saw in nature. Guaranteeing agreeable gathering living in bondage is critical to forestall social pressure, hostility, and expected wounds. Cautious observing of gathering cooperations and the making of viable gatherings are essential parts of moral kangaroo the board.

3. **Conduct Enhancement Difficulties**

Conduct enhancement is principal to the prosperity of hostage kangaroos. Nonetheless, planning powerful advancement exercises that animate normal ways of behaving can challenge. The unique idea of kangaroo ways of behaving, including jumping, rummaging, and preparing, requires a smart way to deal with improvement. Inability to give satisfactory excitement can prompt weariness, stereotypic ways of behaving, and in general reduced government assistance.

III. Wellbeing The executives Difficulties

1. **Illness Transmission in Bondage**

   Hostage conditions, where kangaroos live in closeness, represent an uplifted gamble of sickness transmission. Irresistible infections can spread quickly among people, risking the soundness of the whole populace. Vigorous sickness the executives procedures, including quarantine conventions, normal wellbeing evaluations, and inoculation programs, are fundamental to forestall episodes and keep up with the general strength of hostage kangaroos.

2. **Stress-related Medical problems**
Stress is an unavoidable worry in hostage kangaroo the executives and can appear in different structures, including physiological and social changes. Factors like guest collaborations, changes in friendly elements, and natural aggravations can add to ongoing pressure. Ongoing pressure compromises the safe framework, making kangaroos more vulnerable to infections, wounds, and conceptive issues.

3. **Regenerative Wellbeing Difficulties**

Keeping up with regenerative wellbeing is basic for hostage kangaroo populaces, especially those engaged with rearing projects focused on protection. Difficulties might emerge through rearing hardships, low richness rates, and regenerative illnesses. Guaranteeing ideal conceptive wellbeing requires close observing, veterinary mediation, and, now and again, helped regenerative advancements.

IV. Dietary Contemplations

1. **Dietary Difficulties in Imprisonment**
Giving a healthfully adjusted diet is a key part of kangaroo care in imprisonment. Imitating the different and normal eating regimen of kangaroos presents difficulties, particularly when hostage consumes less calories depend on financially planned takes care of. Guaranteeing that kangaroos get fitting supplements, nutrients, and minerals is urgent for their general wellbeing and conceptive achievement.

2. **Gastrointestinal Wellbeing**

Kangaroos have extraordinary stomach related frameworks adjusted to a stringy, plant-based diet. Unexpected dietary changes, lacking fiber admission, or lopsided characteristics in nourishment can prompt gastrointestinal issues like colic or enteritis. Cautious detailing of diets, thought of individual dietary requirements, and normal observing of gastrointestinal wellbeing are fundamental parts of hostage kangaroo nourishment.

V. Veterinary Consideration and Clinical Intercessions

1. **Particular Veterinary Consideration**
Admittance to specific veterinary consideration is fundamental for tending to medical problems in hostage kangaroos. Veterinarians with skill in marsupial medication are fundamental for leading routine wellbeing checks, diagnosing sicknesses, and giving clinical mediations when essential. Standard wellbeing

appraisals add to the early recognition and the board of potential medical problems.

2. **Analytic Difficulties**

Diagnosing medical problems in kangaroos can be trying because of their novel physiology and ways of behaving. Symptomatic methodology, including blood tests, radiography, and ultrasonography, may require specific methodologies. Progressions in analytic advances and examination on kangaroo wellbeing add to worked on symptomatic precision and treatment results.

3. **Sedation and Sedation Dangers**

Sedation and sedation present intrinsic dangers in any veterinary methodology, and kangaroos are no exemption. Because of their special life structures and physiology, directing sedation to kangaroos requires cautious thought. Checking essential signs, choosing fitting sedative specialists, and limiting pressure during techniques are basic to guaranteeing the security of clinical intercessions.

VI. Ecological and Living space Contemplations

1. **Temperature and Environment Difficulties**

Kangaroos are adjusted to different environments in the wild, and keeping up with ideal natural circumstances in bondage is fundamental for their wellbeing. Outrageous temperatures, lacking asylum, or openness to unfavorable atmospheric conditions can influence the prosperity of hostage kangaroos. Walled in areas should be intended to give warm solace and assurance from ecological stressors.

2. **Territory Advancement and Plan**

Naturalistic environment configuration is significant for advancing the government assistance of hostage kangaroos. Improved conditions that emulate their local living spaces work with normal ways of behaving, mental excitement, and active work. Elements like changed geology, vegetation, and water sources add to the general prosperity of kangaroos in imprisonment.

VII. Moral The travel industry and Public Connection

1. **Guest Effect on Creature Government assistance**

Public collaboration with hostage kangaroos is a typical element in numerous offices. While this gives valuable open doors to training and mindfulness, it additionally presents dangers to the government assistance of the creatures. Excessively excited guests, ill-advised taking care of, and unreasonable commotion can cause pressure and social disturbances among kangaroos. Executing clear rules for guest collaborations and observing guest conduct are fundamental for keeping up with creature government assistance.

2. Adjusting Schooling and Creature Government assistance

Instructive projects focused on guests should work out some kind of harmony between bringing issues to light about kangaroos and guaranteeing the government assistance of the hostage people. Moral the travel industry rehearses, mindful natural life seeing, and powerful correspondence about the necessities and ways of behaving of kangaroos are significant parts of this difficult exercise.

VIII. Preservation Suggestions

1. Hereditary Variety Difficulties

Hostage kangaroo populaces frequently face difficulties connected with hereditary variety. Restricted genetic supplies inside hostage gatherings can prompt inbreeding, lessening the general wellness and versatility of the populace. Hereditary administration systems, like painstakingly arranged reproducing programs and hereditary observing, are fundamental to keep up with hereditary variety and forestall the adverse consequences of inbreeding.

2. Combination with Protection Objectives

The job of hostage kangaroo the board in more extensive preservation objectives requires cautious thought. Guaranteeing that hostage conditions contribute definitively to the protection of wild populaces includes cooperative endeavors between hostage offices and preservation associations. Preservation centered drives, for example, living space rebuilding tasks and local area commitment, upgrade the general effect of hostage kangaroo the board on species protection.

IX. Future Headings and Exploration Needs

1. Headways in Conduct Exploration

Progressions in conduct research are fundamental for acquiring a more profound comprehension of kangaroo ways of behaving, social designs, and ecological inclinations.

Progressing research adds to the advancement of powerful enhancement methodologies, living space plans, and the board rehearses that focus on the social government assistance of hostage kangaroos.

2. Advancements in Veterinary Medication

Proceeded with advancements in veterinary medication are essential for tending to wellbeing challenges in hostage kangaroo populaces. Examination into kangaroo-explicit sicknesses, demonstrative devices, and clinical therapies improves the capacity to give ideal veterinary consideration. Cooperative examination endeavors between veterinarians, researcher, and behaviorists add to a comprehensive way to deal with kangaroo wellbeing and government assistance.

3. Reasonable Practices and Protection Schooling

The eventual fate of kangaroo the executives lies in the reception of feasible practices and a promise to protection schooling. Nooks planned with eco-accommodating standards, natural surroundings joining drives, and instructive projects that encourage a more profound comprehension of kangaroo environment add to the drawn out prosperity of hostage populaces and backing more extensive protection goals.

3.2 Psychological Impact of Captivity

The mental effect of imprisonment on kangaroos is a multi-layered and complex subject that requests a thorough investigation of their conduct reactions, stressors, and procedures for advancing mental prosperity. As marsupials known for their dynamic and social nature, kangaroos in imprisonment might encounter a scope of difficulties that impact their emotional well-being. This examination plans to dig into the mental parts of kangaroo imprisonment, revealing insight into the likely stressors, conduct variations, and measures to improve their mental prosperity.

II. Regular Ways of behaving and Social Designs

1. **Bouncing and Scrounging: Natural Ways of behaving**
   Kangaroos are portrayed by their exceptional headway — bouncing. In the wild, bouncing permits them to cover huge distances proficiently looking for food and water. Hostage conditions, be that as it may, frequently limit the degree of jumping, influencing their capacity to communicate this inborn way of behaving. Giving chances to jumping and rummaging exercises in imprisonment is vital for tending to their normal impulses and advancing mental advancement.

2. **Social Designs and Gathering Living**

Kangaroos are intrinsically friendly creatures, framing complex gathering structures in nature. The elements of these gatherings include various leveled structures, correspondence through non-verbal communication, and helpful ways of behaving. Hostage conditions that neglect to duplicate these social designs might prompt pressure and conduct issues. Understanding and working with regular social collaborations among kangaroos in bondage are fundamental parts of advancing their mental prosperity.

III. Stressors in Hostage Conditions

1. **Space Constraints and Fenced in area Plan**
   The restriction of kangaroos in moderately little nooks can be a huge stressor. In the wild, they have immense home reaches, and the impediments of hostage spaces might limit their regular development designs. Walled in area plan that consolidates open spaces, fluctuated landscape, and regular elements is basic for moderating the pressure related with space limits.

2. **Human Cooperation and Guest Unsettling influences**
   Human connection, particularly in settings where kangaroos are in plain view

for guests, can be a likely stressor. Boisterous clamors, abrupt developments, and direct contact with guests might cause pressure among hostage kangaroos. Laying out rules for mindful guest associations, limiting unsettling influences, and giving segregated regions to withdraw add to lessening feelings of anxiety.

3. **Changes in Friendly Elements**

Adjustments in friendly elements, like the presentation of new people or changes in bunch arrangement, can be wellsprings of stress. Kangaroos might encounter social pecking orders and regional debates, prompting conduct disturbances. Cautious administration of social presentations and checking of overall vibes are fundamental to limit pressure related with changes in friendly designs.

IV. Social Variations in Imprisonment

1. **Stereotypic Ways of behaving**
   One of the mental reactions to imprisonment is the advancement of stereotypic ways of behaving. These tedious, apparently purposeless activities, like pacing or dull bouncing, may arise as methods for dealing with especially difficult times for pressure or fatigue. Stereotypic ways of behaving are characteristic of mental misery and highlight the significance of addressing natural and conduct improvement to forestall their turn of events.

2. **Changed Action Examples**
   In imprisonment, kangaroos might display modified action designs contrasted with their wild partners. Diminished bouncing, expanded rest, or strange ways of behaving can mean the mental effect of imprisonment. Noticing and understanding these progressions are urgent for recognizing possible stressors and executing mediations to help regular action designs.

3. **Hostility and Predominance Presentations**

Changes in friendly elements inside hostage gatherings might prompt hostility and predominance shows. These ways of behaving are reactions to stressors like regional debates or contest for assets. Carrying out methodologies to oversee social communications, giving adequate assets, and offering improvement exercises can assist with moderating hostility and advance a more amicable hostage climate.

V. Procedures for Mental Improvement

1. **Naturalistic Walled in areas**
   Planning naturalistic nooks that duplicate the kangaroos' local living spaces is a principal methodology for mental improvement. Open spaces, various vegetation, and elements that impersonate the normal landscape add to a seriously invigorating climate. Such plans permit kangaroos to communicate their regular ways of behaving, including jumping, brushing, and investigation.

2. **Social Improvement Projects**

Social improvement programs assume a pivotal part in advancing mental prosperity. These projects include the arrangement of intellectually invigorating exercises that support regular ways of behaving. Scavenging open doors, puzzle feeders, and items for control are instances of improvement exercises that connect with kangaroos both intellectually and actually.

3. **Gathering The board**

Understanding the intricacies of social designs and elements is fundamental for successful gathering the board. Cautiously presenting new people, checking bunch communications, and giving open doors to positive social commitment add to a more adjusted and socially enhanced climate.

4. **Hideouts and Retreat Spaces**

Giving hideouts and retreat spaces inside fenced in areas permits kangaroos to have command over their current circumstance. These spaces act as shelters where people can withdraw from social cooperations or guest unsettling influences, decreasing pressure and advancing a feeling that everything is good.

5. **Ecological Variety**

Presenting ecological variety inside hostage spaces forestalls dullness and animates normal ways of behaving. Fluctuating territory, evolving vegetation, and mobile articles give tangible excitement, empowering kangaroos to investigate and draw in with their current circumstance.

VI. Checking and Evaluation

1. **Social Checking**

Normal social observing is a major part of surveying the mental prosperity of hostage kangaroos. Perception of action designs, social connections, and the declaration of normal ways of behaving gives bits of knowledge into their psychological state. Changes in conduct can act as early marks of pressure or other mental issues.

2. **Physiological Markers**

Physiological pointers, for example, cortisol levels and pulse, offer goal proportions of pressure and prosperity. Painless strategies, including waste chemical examination, empower guardians and scientists to evaluate the effect of bondage on kangaroo physiology and carry out designated intercessions in view of these appraisals.

3. **Veterinary Wellbeing Checks**

Ordinary veterinary wellbeing checks are fundamental for distinguishing and addressing any medical problems that might add to mental trouble. Complete wellbeing appraisals, including dental consideration, parasite control, and regenerative wellbeing assessments, guarantee the general prosperity of hostage kangaroo populaces.

VII. Preservation and Training Drives

1. **Preservation Informing**

   Hostage conditions act as strong stages for preservation informing. Instructive projects that feature the difficulties looked by kangaroos in the wild, the significance of their protection, and the job of hostage conditions in supporting species safeguarding add to a feeling of direction and importance for the two guardians and guests.

2. **Research Commitments**

Hostage kangaroo populaces can make significant commitments to logical examination. Concentrates on conduct, proliferation, and wellbeing inside hostage settings give experiences that illuminate more extensive preservation endeavors. Cooperative exploration drives between hostage offices and scholastic foundations improve how we might interpret kangaroo science and conduct.

VIII. Challenges in Tending to Mental Effect

1. **Space Restrictions in Imprisonment**

   Notwithstanding endeavors to make naturalistic nooks, space constraints in imprisonment stay a huge test. Hostage conditions might in all likelihood never completely repeat the immense territories of the wild, restricting the degree to which kangaroos can communicate specific ways of behaving. Offsetting space imperatives with improvement procedures is a continuous test.

2. **Guest Creature Connections**

   The presence of guests and the related connections present difficulties for dealing with the mental effect on kangaroos. Finding some kind of harmony between instructive open doors and limiting pressure from guest unsettling influences requires cautious preparation, clear rules, and continuous training for guests.

3. **Restricted Exploration on Kangaroo Conduct**

Contrasted with a few different animal groups, there is a generally restricted collection of examination on kangaroo conduct, particularly in bondage. Further exploration is expected to extend how we might interpret their mental capacities, correspondence examples, and reactions to different natural improvements. This information is crucial for fitting improvement programs and further developing hostage the executives rehearses.

IX. Future Bearings in Hostage Kangaroo The executives

1. **Headways in Social Exploration**
   Headways in social examination, including mental examinations and evaluations of profound prosperity, will add to a more nuanced comprehension of kangaroo brain science. Investigating the mental capacities of kangaroos and their reactions to various types of enhancement will illuminate more designated and successful techniques.
2. **Advancement in Nook Plan**
   Proceeded with advancement in nook configuration is pivotal for tending to the mental effect of bondage. Coordinating innovation, like augmented simulation or intuitive highlights, and investigating new materials that mirror normal substrates can upgrade the tactile encounters of kangaroos in imprisonment.
3. **Joint effort for Protection**

The fate of hostage kangaroo the executives lies in cooperative endeavors between offices, protection associations, and examination foundations. Sharing information, information, and best practices can add to the advancement of normalized rules for kangaroo the executives, guaranteeing the prosperity of hostage populaces and adjusting endeavors to more extensive protection objectives.

3.3 Reproductive Challenges in Captive Settings

Regenerative difficulties in hostage kangaroo settings present a diverse arrangement of issues that request cautious thought and vital administration. Kangaroos, with their one of a kind conceptive physiology and social designs, may confront impediments to fruitful reproducing in imprisonment. This investigation dives into the intricacies of regenerative difficulties, inspecting variables, for example, rearing troubles, low ripeness rates, and conceptive illnesses. Understanding these difficulties is essential for the improvement of viable techniques to help effective reproducing programs in hostage conditions.

II. Exceptional Conceptive Physiology

1. **Undeveloped Diapause**
   Kangaroos display an unmistakable regenerative peculiarity known as early stage diapause. In contrast to most warm blooded animals, where the advancement of the undeveloped organism continues persistently, kangaroos can defer the movement of early stage improvement until outer circumstances are great. In imprisonment, the guideline of this diapause and its synchronization with ecological signs present difficulties for reproducing achievement.
2. **Postponed Implantation**

Postponed implantation is one more remarkable part of kangaroo proliferation. Following mating, the undeveloped organism goes through a time of suspended improvement prior to embedding in the uterus. Understanding and controlling this cycle in hostage settings is basic for effective rearing, as the planning of implantation straightforwardly impacts the development time frame and birth timing.

III. Social and Conduct Elements

1. **Social Progressive system and Reproducing Achievement**

   Kangaroos are social creatures with progressive gathering structures. In hostage settings, keeping up with normal social elements is essential for fruitful rearing. Prevailing people might corner mating valuable open doors, prompting difficulties in guaranteeing conceptive accomplishment for all individuals from the gathering. Cautious administration of social designs and giving open doors to less prevailing people are fundamental contemplations.

2. **Regional Ways of behaving and Reproducing Domains**

In the wild, kangaroos display regional ways of behaving, with prevailing guys laying out rearing domains. Hostage conditions might present difficulties in repeating these normal ways of behaving. Presenting controlled rearing domains inside nooks and overseeing regional associations are methodologies to address this part of kangaroo propagation in bondage.

IV. Social Pressure and Conceptive Wellbeing

1. **Stress-Initiated Conceptive Concealment**

   Stress is a huge element impacting conceptive progress in kangaroos. Changes in friendly elements, ecological aggravations, or disturbances brought about by human cooperations can prompt pressure, prompting regenerative concealment. Distinguishing and alleviating stressors through natural advancement and cautious administration rehearses are fundamental for advancing conceptive wellbeing.

2. **Effect of Imprisonment on Mating Ways of behaving**

The restricted spaces of hostage conditions might impact regular mating ways of behaving. Kangaroos might encounter difficulties in communicating romance ways of behaving, sex, or mate choice. Noticing and understanding these ways of behaving in bondage is critical for distinguishing likely boundaries to fruitful rearing and executing mediations to work with regular mating processes.

V. Infection Related Regenerative Difficulties

1. **Regenerative Parcel Diseases**

   Regenerative parcel diseases can present critical difficulties to kangaroo rearing in imprisonment. Diseases in guys or females can affect ripeness and regenerative achievement. Normal veterinary wellbeing checks, observing for indications of conceptive plot contaminations, and carrying out proper clinical mediations are fundamental parts of overseeing infection related regenerative difficulties.

2. Effect of Weight on Conceptive Sicknesses

Stress is a contributing component to the powerlessness of kangaroos to conceptive sicknesses. Ongoing pressure debilitates the safe framework, making people more powerless against diseases. Along these lines, tending to pressure through legitimate administration rehearses, natural enhancement, and conduct support is essential for forestalling and overseeing conceptive illnesses.

VI. Low Fruitfulness Rates and Reproducing Challenges

1. Hereditary Variety and Inbreeding

Keeping up with hereditary variety inside hostage kangaroo populaces is fundamental for forestalling inbreeding, which can prompt decreased fruitfulness rates and expanded defenselessness to hereditary problems. Hereditary administration methodologies, including cautious matching of people and hereditary checking, are critical for supporting solid and feasible hostage populaces.

2. Age-Related Ripeness Decline

Female kangaroos might encounter age-related decreases in ripeness, especially as they arrive at the later phases of their conceptive life expectancy. Cautious thought of the age and conceptive history of people is fundamental while arranging rearing projects. Checking and changing rearing systems in light old enough related factors add to better regenerative results.

VII. Regenerative Administration Methodologies

1. Hormonal Checking and Intercession

Hormonal checking is a significant device in conceptive administration. Evaluating chemical levels in females can give bits of knowledge into their conceptive status, including the planning of estrus and potential issues influencing ripeness. Hormonal mediations, like the utilization of regenerative chemicals or planned impregnation, might be considered to upgrade reproducing achievement.

2. Ecological Improvement for Stress Decrease

Ecological enhancement assumes an essential part in lessening pressure and elevating normal ways of behaving helpful for effective rearing. Giving differed scenes, concealing spots, and potential open doors for social connections add to a less upsetting climate. Enhancement exercises that animate mental and actual prosperity can emphatically influence regenerative wellbeing.

3. Reproducing Season Reenactment

Recreating normal rearing seasons inside hostage conditions adjusts regenerative ways of behaving to natural signs. Controlling lighting conditions, temperature, and other natural variables can add to the synchronization of rearing cycles among people, improving the probability of fruitful mating and proliferation.

4. **Cautious Matching and Social Elements The board**

Matching people cautiously, taking into account factors like hereditary variety, age, and social similarity, is critical for effective rearing. Checking and overseeing social elements inside bunches forestall strength related difficulties and guarantee that all people have equivalent open doors for mating.

VIII. Coordinated effort and Exploration Drives

1. **Coordinated effort Between Offices**
   Coordinated effort between various hostage offices is fundamental for sharing information, encounters, and hereditary assets. Laying out networks for the trading of people, hereditary data, and best practices adds to the general progress of kangaroo rearing projects.

2. **Research on Conceptive Physiology**
   Proceeded with investigation into kangaroo conceptive physiology upgrades how we might interpret their special regenerative instruments. Exploring the complexities of undeveloped diapause, postponed implantation, and hormonal guideline gives significant experiences to refining conceptive administration methodologies.

3. **Long haul Observing and Information Assortment**

Long haul checking of hostage populaces, including conceptive narratives, well-being records, and social perceptions, adds to the aggregation of important information. Examining patterns and examples over the long haul empowers guardians and scientists to distinguish difficulties, evaluate the outcome of intercessions, and adjust the executives techniques appropriately.

IX. Moral Contemplations in Conceptive Administration

1. **Offsetting Conceptive Objectives with Government assistance**
   Offsetting regenerative objectives with the government assistance of individual kangaroos is a fundamental moral thought. Guaranteeing that reproducing programs focus on the prosperity of the creatures, limit pressure, and give open doors to regular ways of behaving is fundamental for mindful hostage the board.

2. **Limits of Hostage Conditions**

Perceiving the inborn constraints of hostage conditions is pivotal in laying out sensible assumptions for conceptive achievement. While endeavors can be made to duplicate regular circumstances, certain parts of kangaroo conceptive way of behaving might be trying to completely communicate in imprisonment.

Chapter 4

Enrichment Strategies For Captive Kangaroos

Improvement is an essential part of mindful hostage kangaroo the board, meaning to upgrade the physical and mental prosperity of people. Hostage conditions, while fundamental for protection and instructive purposes, can introduce difficulties in duplicating the intricacy of nature. This extensive investigation dives into a horde of improvement systems intended to address the extraordinary ways of behaving, social designs, and ecological inclinations of kangaroos. From living space plan and social connections to mental excitement and active work, these procedures expect to advance a satisfying and normal life for kangaroos in imprisonment.

II. Figuring out Regular Ways of behaving

1. **Bouncing and Investigation**

   One of the characterizing elements of kangaroos is their unmistakable jumping velocity. Giving extensive and changed scenes inside nooks permits kangaroos to communicate their normal bouncing ways of behaving. Integrating lopsided landscape, verdant regions, and impediments empowers investigation, copying the unique conditions of their wild partners.

2. **Scrounging and Touching**

   Kangaroos are herbivores with a specific stomach related framework adjusted for a plant-based diet. Offering valuable open doors for searching and brushing is critical for their actual wellbeing and mental feeling. Presenting local vegetation, peruse materials, and decisively positioned food sources empowers normal taking care of ways of behaving, adding to an even eating routine.

3. **Social Collaborations and Overall vibes**

In the wild, kangaroos are social creatures with complex gathering structures. Duplicating these social elements in bondage is fundamental for their prosperity. Cautiously overseeing gatherings, taking into account viable people, and giving spaces to social connections encourage a feeling of local area, lessening pressure and advancing regular ways of behaving.

III. Ecological Improvement

1. **Naturalistic Nooks**
   Planning walled in areas that reflect the kangaroos' regular natural surroundings is fundamental for ecological improvement. Counting highlights like local vegetation, shakes, and water components adds to an outwardly invigorating climate. Changed geography, including slopes and inclines, adds intricacy to the landscape, empowering active work and investigation.

2. **Asylum and Retreat Spaces**
   Making protected regions inside nooks permits kangaroos to withdraw from outrageous weather patterns, giving them a feeling that everything is good. These spaces additionally act as hideouts where people can rest or participate in singular exercises, lining up with their normal ways of behaving.

3. **Portable and Rotatable Articles**

Presenting versatile and rotatable items, like logs, rocks, and stages, adds an intuitive component to the climate. Kangaroos can control these items, advancing actual work and mental commitment. The capacity to revamp components inside the climate improves their feeling of control and decision.

IV. Mental Enhancement

1. **Puzzle Feeders and Food Gadgets**
   Mental enhancement is fundamental for invigorating the personalities of hostage kangaroos. Puzzle feeders and food gadgets challenge them to issue tackle and utilize their mental capacities to get to food rewards. Covering food inside items or gadgets energizes investigation and draws in their normal critical thinking impulses.

2. **Tangible Improvements**
   Drawing in numerous faculties is significant for exhaustive enhancement. Presenting tangible upgrades like aromas, sounds, and material components adds intricacy to the climate. Fragrance trails, recorded regular sounds, and finished surfaces give tangible variety, improving the general enhancement experience.

3. **Novel Items and Curiosity**

Kangaroos are normally inquisitive creatures, and openness to novel items supports investigation and premium. Presenting new things, fragrances, or designs on a turning premise forestalls adjustment and keeps up with the oddity factor, keeping the improvement experience drawing in and dynamic.

V. Actual work and Exercise

1. **Hindrance Courses and Deftness Designs**
   Giving open doors to actual work is fundamental for the wellbeing and prosperity of kangaroos. Planning deterrent courses and readiness structures inside nooks energizes bouncing, hopping, and climbing. These exercises imitate their normal developments, advancing cardiovascular wellness and solid strength.
2. **Water Elements and Swimming Open doors**
   While not all kangaroo species are known for their abilities to swim, some, similar to the red kangaroo, can swim. Consolidating shallow water elements or pools permits kangaroos to participate in water-related exercises. Indeed, even species that don't swim can profit from admittance to water for drinking and swimming.
3. **Toys and Play Designs**

Giving toys and play structures adds a component of tomfoolery and play to the climate. Objects like balls, hanging things, or designs that energize communication can animate play ways of behaving. Play isn't just actually valuable yet in addition adds to social associations among people.

VI. Taking care of Enhancement

1. **Assortment in Diet**
   Repeating the variety of a wild eating routine is vital for hostage kangaroo sustenance. Offering an assortment of peruse materials, leaves, organic products, and vegetables guarantees a balanced eating regimen. Also, pivoting food things presents assortment and forestalls dullness, empowering normal taking care of ways of behaving.
2. **Rummaging Open doors**
   Setting out open doors for rummaging draws in kangaroos in a more naturalistic taking care of involvement. Dissipate taking care of, where food is spread across the nook, or concealing food inside substrates like straw or leaves urges them to utilize their faculties and rummaging impulses to find and eat their feasts.
3. **Taking care of Time Changeability**

Changing the timing and strategies for taking care of adds unconventionality to their everyday daily schedule. Kangaroos in the wild don't have a proper timetable for food accessibility, so presenting fluctuation in taking care of times and strategies lines up with their normal encounters, advancing mental feeling.

VII. Social Enhancement

1. **Viable Gatherings**
   Guaranteeing similarity inside gatherings is pivotal for the outcome of social improvement. Noticing social elements, overseeing presentations cautiously,

and giving open doors to positive cooperations add to the general prosperity of kangaroos in social environments.

2. **Presenting New People**

Acquainting new people with gatherings adds a unique component to their current circumstance. Cautious preparation, checking, and continuous presentations assist with forestalling pressure and animosity. Positive social collaborations, like preparing or playing, add to an agreeable general vibe.

3. **Conceptive Open doors**

For species associated with rearing projects, working with conceptive open doors lines up with normal ways of behaving. Overseeing rearing seasons, establishing proper reproducing conditions, and checking people for indications of estrus or romance ways of behaving add to both conceptive and social enhancement.

VIII. Veterinary Consideration and Wellbeing Checks

1. **Positive Veterinary Associations**

Advancing positive relationship with veterinary consideration is fundamental for the general prosperity of hostage kangaroos. Consolidating encouraging feedback strategies during wellbeing checks and operations diminishes pressure and cultivates a helpful connection between the creatures and guardians.

2. **Routine Wellbeing Checks and Observing**

Normal veterinary wellbeing checks are essential to preventive consideration. Observing individual wellbeing, dental circumstances, and addressing any medical problems instantly add to the generally physical and mental prosperity of hostage kangaroos.

IX. Difficulties and Contemplations

1. **Adjusting Oddity and Adjustment**

While presenting novel components is critical, overseers should figure out some kind of harmony to forestall adjustment. Routinely pivoting enhancement things, fluctuating the planning of presentations, and cautiously noticing individual reactions assist with keeping up with the oddity factor.

2. **Individual Variety in Inclinations**

Understanding that singular kangaroos might have special inclinations is fundamental. A few people might incline toward specific sorts of enhancement over others. Noticing and adjusting improvement methodologies in view of individual reactions add to customized and compelling enhancement plans.

X. Future Headings in Advancement

1. **Headways in Social Exploration**
   Headways in social exploration add to a more profound comprehension of kangaroo cognizance, inclinations, and reactions to improvement. Continuous examinations on mental capacities, tangible insight, and individual varieties illuminate the advancement regarding more custom fitted and compelling improvement systems.
2. **Mechanical Combination**
   Investigating the coordination of innovation in improvement methodologies presents energizing prospects. Computer generated reality reenactments, intelligent gadgets, and sensor-based frameworks can improve the intricacy of the enhancement experience, giving extra layers of feeling to hostage kangaroos.
3. **Coordinated effort and Information Sharing**

The fate of improvement methodologies for hostage kangaroos lies in cooperation and information dividing between offices and specialists. Laying out networks for sharing victories, difficulties, and developments guarantees an aggregate exertion toward refining and propelling improvement rehearses.

4.1 Physical Enrichment

Actual improvement assumes a crucial part in the prosperity of hostage kangaroos by empowering regular developments, animating actual wellness, and supporting in general wellbeing. In their local natural surroundings, kangaroos are known for their unmistakable bouncing, hopping, and climbing ways of behaving. In imprisonment, reproducing these regular exercises is urgent for guaranteeing the physical and emotional wellness of these notorious marsupials. This thorough investigation dives into different actual advancement techniques intended to address the exceptional velocity, outer muscle wellbeing, and regular ways of behaving of kangaroos in hostage settings.

II. Figuring out Kangaroo Velocity

1. **Jumping as a Characteristic Way of behaving**
   Jumping is the essential method of motion for kangaroos in nature. It fills different needs, including covering huge distances proficiently, keeping away from hunters, and arriving at food and water sources.
   Hostage conditions should work with jumping to permit kangaroos to communicate this normal way of behaving, advancing actual work and cardiovascular wellbeing.
2. **Influence on Outer muscle Framework**

The outer muscle arrangement of kangaroos is adjusted to the requests of bouncing. Their strong rear appendages and solid tail give the essential impetus to this novel type of velocity. Repeating bouncing exercises in imprisonment is fundamental for keeping up with the soundness of their muscles, bones, and joints. Absence of proper actual work can prompt muscle decay, joint firmness, and other medical problems.

III. Open air Nooks and Differed Territory

1. **Far reaching Open air Spaces**
   Planning nooks that give sweeping outside spaces is principal for advancing regular movement. Huge regions permit kangaroos to bounce unreservedly, mirroring the immense scenes of their local territories. Far reaching walled in areas additionally add to the declaration of other regular ways of behaving, like brushing, searching, and social connections.

2. **Fluctuated Territory and Geography**
   Consolidating changed landscape inside outside walled in areas adds intricacy to the climate. Slopes, slants, and lopsided surfaces animate different muscle gatherings and draw in the kangaroos in a scope of developments. This variety reflects the regular scenes where kangaroos explore different landscapes in nature.

3. **Normal Substrates for Effect Assimilation**

Giving normal substrates like soil or grass in open air fenced in areas assimilates the effect of jumping. Kangaroos are adjusted to arrive on delicate surfaces, and the utilization of normal substrates lessens the gamble of outer muscle wounds. It additionally improves the tangible experience for the kangaroos, permitting them to really draw in with the climate more.

IV. Fake Designs and Hindrance Courses

1. **Fake Designs for Climbing**
   While bouncing is a dominating way of behaving, kangaroos likewise take part in climbing exercises, particularly in rough territories. Presenting fake designs like climbing stages, shakes, and logs inside walled in areas empowers climbing ways of behaving. Climbing gives actual activity as well as animates mental commitment as kangaroos plan their developments.

2. **Obstruction Courses for Dexterity**
   Planning snag courses inside walled in areas fills in as a powerful system for advancing deftness and coordination. Consolidating obstacles, stages, and passages moves kangaroos to imaginatively explore the climate. Nimbleness based exercises add to the advancement of coordinated movements and forestall actual stagnation.

3. **Manipulable Articles for Communication**

Objects that kangaroos can control act as both physical and mental enhancement. Things like hanging logs, versatile designs, or articles that energize moving around connect with different muscle gatherings. Intelligent articles likewise add a component of play to the climate, advancing actual work through investigation and control.

V. Water Highlights and Sea-going Open doors

1. **Shallow Pools for Swimming**
   Certain kangaroo species, similar to the red kangaroo, can swim and may profit from shallow pools for swimming. Presenting water highlights inside walled in areas gives amazing open doors to kangaroos to participate in water-related exercises. Swimming advances joint adaptability, cooling during warm climate, and fills in as an extra type of actual activity.

2. **Water-Available Stages**
   Stages set inside shallow pools permit kangaroos to get to water at various levels. These stages energize jumping, climbing, and adjusting exercises as kangaroos explore all through the water. Water-open stages add to actual enhancement by joining regular ways of behaving with ecological intricacy.

3. **Hydrotherapy for Recovery**

In instances of injury or recovery, hydrotherapy can be utilized as a designated actual improvement technique. Shallow pools with controlled water levels give a low-influence climate to kangaroos to practice and recuperate. Hydrotherapy upholds muscle strength, joint versatility, and in general recovery endeavors.

VI. Play Designs and Toys

1. **Ball Play for Actual Commitment**
   Presenting chunks of different sizes empowers play ways of behaving that include kicking, pushing, and pursuing. Ball play isn't just a wellspring of actual activity yet additionally invigorates coordination and muscle commitment. Rolling or bobbing balls give dynamic improvements that get normal reactions from kangaroos.

2. **Hanging and Suspended Toys**
   Suspended toys or protests that kangaroos can reach and cooperate with while standing or jumping add to actual advancement. These things support extending, coming to, and vertical development, drawing in various muscle gatherings. The powerful idea of hanging toys adds unconventionality to the climate, advancing mental excitement too.

3. **Structures for Climbing and Hopping**

Specially crafted climbing structures inside fenced in areas give amazing open doors to kangaroos to participate in climbing and bouncing exercises. Stages, inclines, and raised structures support vertical development and dynamic actual effort. Climbing structures likewise act as vantage focuses for kangaroos to review their environmental factors.

VII. Occasional Variety and Ecological Changes

1. **Occasional Changes for Conduct Variety**
   Consolidating occasional varieties in the climate adds a component of unconventionality and social variety. Changes in vegetation, climate, or the presentation of occasional components give novel upgrades that energize investigation and variation. Occasional improvement techniques line up with the regular variances kangaroos experience in nature.

2. **Temperature Variety for Variation**
   Making temperature varieties inside walled in areas permits kangaroos to adjust to various circumstances. This can incorporate regions with conceal for blistering climate and shielded spaces for colder temperatures. Giving temperature-fitting substrates likewise urges kangaroos to pick regions that best suit their solace, advancing normal ways of behaving.

3. **Pivot of Advancement Components**

Consistently turning and presenting new components inside the walled in area forestalls adjustment and keeps up with interest. Kangaroos are normally inquisitive, and the presentation of novel components empowers investigation and commitment. A unique climate with changing components gives progressing physical and mental excitement.

VIII. Cooperative Social Open doors

1. **Bunch Play and Social Connections**
   Working with bunch play among kangaroos upgrades actual commitment and social cooperations. Kangaroos frequently participate in play ways of behaving with conspecifics, including pursuing, kicking, and delicate wrestling.
   Empowering positive social cooperations adds to the general prosperity of people inside a social environment.

2. **Presenting Viable People**
   Acquainting new people with gatherings gives potential open doors to socialization and shared proactive tasks. Painstakingly oversaw presentations forestall pressure and advance positive collaborations. Overall vibes add to the improvement of social bonds, lessening the gamble of social segregation.

3. **Regenerative Open doors for Social Communication**

For species engaged with rearing projects, giving open doors to regenerative communications lines up with normal ways of behaving. Making spaces helpful for romance, mating, and nurturing ways of behaving upholds social improvement.

Cautious administration of reproducing amazing open doors adds to the general wellbeing and essentialness of hostage kangaroo populaces.

IX. Wellbeing Checking and Veterinarian Cooperation

1. **Ordinary Wellbeing Checks for Preventive Consideration**

   Observing the strength of kangaroos is critical for forestalling and resolving actual issues. Ordinary wellbeing checks, including outer muscle evaluations, add to preventive consideration. Recognizing any indications of injury or uneasiness takes into consideration convenient mediations to help actual prosperity.

2. **Coordinated effort with Veterinarians for Recovery**

In instances of injury or wellbeing concerns, coordinated effort with veterinarians is fundamental for creating recovery plans. Actual advancement procedures can be customized to help the particular necessities of kangaroos going through recovery. Veterinary info guarantees that the picked exercises line up with recuperation objectives.

X. Difficulties and Contemplations

1. **Individual Variety in Actual Capacities**

   Perceiving that singular kangaroos might have shifting actual capacities is fundamental. A people might show constraints because old enough, injury, or medical issue. Advancement plans ought to be versatile to oblige individual requirements, guaranteeing that all kangaroos can take part in proactive tasks at their own speed.

2. **Adjusting Force and Security**

While actual enhancement means to give drawing in exercises, security is fundamental. Adjusting the force of exercises with security contemplations forestalls wounds and stress. Noticing kangaroo reactions and changing improvement components in light of their solace levels adds to a positive and secure climate.

XI. Future Bearings in Actual Improvement

1. **Mechanical Incorporation for Observing**

   Progressions in innovation offer open doors for observing and upgrading actual improvement. Sensor-based frameworks and GPS beacons can give bits of knowledge into kangaroo developments, action levels, and inclinations. Coordinating innovation permits guardians to unequivocally tailor enhancement procedures more.

2. **Research on Outer muscle Wellbeing**

   Proceeded with research on kangaroo outer muscle wellbeing advises the improvement regarding designated advancement methodologies. Understanding the effect of different exercises on muscle tone, joint wellbeing, and in general actual wellness adds to confirm based rehearses for advancing long haul prosperity.

3. **Advancements in Climbing Designs and Stages**

Investigating imaginative plans for climbing designs and stages improves the actual intricacy of kangaroo conditions. Structures that copy normal components like trees or shake arrangements give chances to climbing and bouncing that intently line up with their ways of behaving in nature.

4.2Social Enrichment

Social enhancement is a foundation of hostage kangaroo the executives, perceiving the inborn social nature of these marsupials. In their normal territories, kangaroos flourish in complex social designs that add to their general prosperity. At the point when in imprisonment, repeating these social elements becomes fundamental for cultivating positive ways of behaving, lessening pressure, and advancing a satisfying life. This investigation dives into different social improvement procedures intended to address the one of a kind social ways of behaving, overall vibes, and correspondence examples of kangaroos in hostage settings.

II. Figuring out Kangaroo Social Ways of behaving

1. **Social Design in Nature**
   Kangaroos are known for their multifaceted social designs that change among species. They structure gatherings, frequently alluded to as hordes or troops, which can go from little nuclear families to bigger accumulations.
   Social cooperations incorporate preparing, playing, and shared assurance inside the gathering. Imitating these regular ways of behaving in imprisonment is urgent for the generally speaking mental and profound strength of kangaroos.

2. **Significance of Social Bonds**

Social bonds among kangaroos fill different needs, from giving security against hunters to working with regenerative exercises. These securities are based on trust, correspondence, and a mutual perspective of collective vibes. In bondage, establishing a climate that upholds the turn of events and support of social bonds is vital.

III. Collective vibes in Hostage Conditions

1. **Bunch Arrangement and Similarity**
   Cautious thought of gathering arrangement is crucial for fruitful social improvement. Kangaroos have individual characters, and similarity inside gatherings impacts their prosperity. Noticing social elements, overseeing presentations continuously, and giving open doors to positive connections add to the advancement of strong gatherings.

2. **Social Order and Strength**
   In the same way as other social creatures, kangaroos lay out progressive systems inside gatherings. Strength and accommodation ways of behaving are normal parts of their social construction. In imprisonment, understanding and regarding social orders are critical for keeping up with bunch solidness and forestalling clashes.

3. **Working with Positive Social Associations**

Advancing positive social collaborations includes establishing a climate helpful for shared preparing, play, and collective exercises. Improvement procedures that urge bunch commitment add to the general prosperity of kangaroos. Giving spaces to shared resting, taking care of, and play upholds the improvement of positive social ways of behaving.

IV. Outside Fenced in areas and Naturalistic Conditions

1. **Broad Spaces for Mingling**
   Planning outside fenced in areas with more than adequate space permits kangaroos to take part in regular social ways of behaving. Sweeping regions empower bouncing, playing, and associating without the imperatives of restricted spaces. Open air conditions additionally add to the statement of regional and exploratory ways of behaving.

2. **Assortment in Territory and Scenes**
   Integrating changed territory inside open air walled in areas adds intricacy to the climate. Various surfaces, inclines, and concealing spots mirror the normal scenes where kangaroos lay out regions and explore assorted territories. Such elements give open doors to investigation and regional collaborations.

3. **Local Vegetation and Scrounging Potential open doors**

Presenting local vegetation inside walled in areas offers both physical and social improvement. Kangaroos can touch together, share taking care of regions, and participate in friendly scavenging. The presence of plants additionally gives visual obstructions, permitting people to take part in normal find the stowaway ways of behaving, adding to overall vibes.

V. Social Groupings and Viable Pairings

1. **Perception of Individual Ways of behaving**
   Understanding the singular ways of behaving of kangaroos is urgent for shaping viable social groupings. Noticing their cooperations, correspondence styles, and inclinations helps with recognizing people that are probably going to frame positive social bonds. Conduct perceptions guide guardians in making amicable social groupings.

2. **Match Holding and Viable Matches**
Some kangaroo species display pair-holding ways of behaving, where people structure close bonds with explicit colleagues. Distinguishing viable matches for socialization is fundamental for those species. Match reinforced kangaroos take part in common preparing, resting together, and supporting each other inwardly.

3. **Presenting New People Steadily**

Acquainting new people with existing gatherings should be done steadily to limit pressure and possible struggles. Controlled acquaintances permit kangaroos with lay out new friendly associations and progressive systems normally. Checking their ways of behaving during presentations guarantees a smooth incorporation into the gathering.

VI. Ecological Improvement for Social Association

1. **Social Spaces and Resting Regions**
Planning conditions that work with social cooperations incorporates giving spaces to shared resting. Kangaroos frequently rest together in closeness, building up friendly bonds. Concealed regions, normal substrates, and decisively positioned structures support bunch rest and unwinding.

2. **Intuitive Designs for Play**
Presenting structures that work with intuitive play among kangaroos adds to social advancement. Climbing structures, hanging things, and toys energize play ways of behaving, for example, pursuing, wrestling, and jumping together. Play serves as an active work as well as for the purpose of building up friendly bonds.

3. **Preparing and Allogrooming Potential open doors**

Preparing is a major social way of behaving among kangaroos. Giving spaces and substrates that permit prepping, or allogrooming (preparing one another), upholds the improvement of social securities. Prepping adds to cleanliness, stress decrease, and the fortifying of social associations.

VII. Regenerative Open doors and Parental Bonds

1. **Working with Regenerative Ways of behaving**
For kangaroo species engaged with rearing projects, establishing conditions helpful for regenerative ways of behaving is essential for social enhancement. This incorporates giving fitting spaces to romance, mating, and settling. Perceiving and supporting normal conceptive ways of behaving adds to in general prosperity.

2. **Supporting Parental Bonds**
Parental consideration is a critical part of kangaroo social design. Kangaroo

moms convey and nurture their joeys in a pocket, and later, the joey keeps on remaining nearby the mother. Empowering normal nurturing ways of behaving, giving protection to holding, and making secure spaces for joey advancement add to the prosperity of parent and posterity.

3. **Collective vibes with Posterity**

In gatherings with joeys, collective vibes shift with the presence of posterity. Noticing and regarding the elements among grown-ups and adolescents is vital for social enhancement. Empowering positive connections and giving spaces where joeys can mingle add to their social turn of events.

VIII. Occasional Varieties and Conduct Variety

1. **Occasional Changes for Conduct Variety**
Presenting occasional changes inside hostage conditions adds conduct variety to social connections. Changes in vegetation, climate, and the accessibility of assets make novel upgrades, empowering investigation and variation. Occasional varieties line up with the normal changes that kangaroos experience in nature.

2. **Temperature Varieties for Variation**
Making temperature varieties inside walled in areas permits kangaroos to adjust to various circumstances. This incorporates giving concealed regions to blistering climate and protected spaces during colder temperatures. Offering temperature-proper substrates additionally urges kangaroos to pick regions that best suit their solace, advancing normal social ways of behaving.

3. **Turn of Improvement Components**

Routinely pivoting and presenting new components inside the fenced in area forestalls adjustment and keeps up with interest. Kangaroos are normally inquisitive, and the presentation of novel components energizes investigation and commitment. A unique climate with changing components gives progressing social and mental excitement.

IX. Cooperative Social Open doors

1. **Bunch Play and Social Associations**
Working with bunch play among kangaroos upgrades social commitment and proactive tasks. Kangaroos frequently participate in play ways of behaving with conspecifics, including pursuing, kicking, and delicate wrestling. Empowering positive social connections adds to the general prosperity of people inside a social environment.

2. **Presenting Viable People**
Acquainting new people with gatherings gives valuable open doors to socialization and shared exercises. Painstakingly oversaw presentations forestall pressure

and advance positive associations. Collective vibes add to the advancement of social bonds, decreasing the gamble of social disconnection.

3. **Regenerative Open doors for Social Connection**

For species engaged with rearing projects, giving open doors to conceptive associations lines up with normal ways of behaving. Making spaces helpful for romance, mating, and nurturing ways of behaving upholds social improvement. Cautious administration of rearing open doors adds to the general wellbeing and imperativeness of hostage kangaroo populaces.

X. Wellbeing Observing and Veterinary Joint effort

1. **Customary Wellbeing Checks for Preventive Consideration**
   Observing the soundness of kangaroos is vital for forestalling and resolving social and actual issues. Normal wellbeing checks, including social appraisals, add to preventive consideration. Distinguishing any indications of stress, animosity, or social moves considers ideal mediations to help their prosperity.

2. **Cooperation with Veterinarians for Conduct Concerns**

In instances of social worries, joint effort with veterinarians is fundamental. Veterinarians can give bits of knowledge into stress-related ways of behaving, social struggles, or different difficulties. Cooperative endeavors guarantee that conduct intercessions line up with the general wellbeing and government assistance of kangaroos.

XI. Difficulties and Contemplations

1. **Individual Variety in Friendly Inclinations**
   Perceiving that singular kangaroos might have differing social inclinations is fundamental. A few people might lean toward isolation, while others flourish in bigger gatherings. Understanding and regarding individual contrasts add to the improvement of custom fitted social enhancement plans.

2. **Adjusting Social Connections and Isolation**

While social connections are urgent, giving open doors to isolation is similarly significant. A few kangaroos might require calm spaces to withdraw and rest. Offsetting social commitment with amazing open doors for isolation guarantees that every individual's social requirements are met.

XII. Future Bearings in Friendly Improvement

1. **Progressions in Social Exploration**
   Proceeded with progressions in conduct research add to a more profound comprehension of kangaroo social elements. Progressing concentrates on

correspondence, individual inclinations, and the effect of social advancement educate the improvement regarding more nuanced and compelling techniques.

2. **Mechanical Mix for Checking Social Collaborations**

Investigating the mix of innovation for checking social connections presents energizing prospects. Sensor-based frameworks, cameras, and GPS beacons can give bits of knowledge into collective vibes, correspondence examples, and individual inclinations. Innovation supports refining social enhancement methodologies in view of ongoing information.

3. **Coordinated effort and Information Sharing**

The eventual fate of social advancement for hostage kangaroos lies in cooperation and information dividing between offices, specialists, and overseers. Laying out networks for sharing triumphs, difficulties, and developments guarantees an aggregate exertion toward refining and propelling social enhancement rehearses.

4.3 Cognitive Enrichment

Mental advancement for hostage kangaroos includes animating their scholarly capacities and advancing mental prosperity. Through exercises like riddle feeders, tangible upgrades, and openness to novel articles, kangaroos participate in critical thinking and investigation. These procedures emulate the difficulties of their common habitat, empowering mental turn of events. Consolidating innovation and progressions in social exploration further upgrades mental enhancement, guaranteeing a dynamic and animating mental scene for hostage kangaroos. Improving their psyches is necessary to cultivating a feeling of interest, versatility, and generally mental wellbeing in bondage.

Chapter 5

Conservation And Educational Roles

Hostage kangaroo the executives assumes a urgent part in protection endeavors and instructive drives, adding to the figuring out, conservation, and enthusiasm for these notorious marsupials. This thorough investigation digs into the double jobs of hostage kangaroo programs, underlining their importance in preservation, logical examination, and government funded training.

II. Preservation Importance

1. **Safeguarding Hereditary Variety**
   Hostage kangaroo populaces act as supplies of hereditary variety, defending exceptional hereditary characteristics that might be essential for the endurance of explicit species. With some kangaroo species confronting dangers in the wild, hostage reproducing programs go about as hereditary wellbeing nets, forestalling the deficiency of important hereditary material.

2. **Species Recuperation and Renewed introduction**
   Kangaroo species that are jeopardized or face natural surroundings misfortune benefit from hostage rearing projects focused on species recuperation and renewed introduction. Laying out practical hostage populaces takes into account painstakingly oversaw renewed introduction endeavors, reestablishing kangaroo populaces to their normal environments and guaranteeing the drawn out endurance of these species.

3. **Hereditary Administration and Reproducing Projects**

Hereditary administration inside hostage populaces is a basic part of preservation endeavors. Keeping up with solid hereditary variety, staying away from inbreeding, and carrying out essential rearing projects add to the general wellness and versatility of hostage kangaroo populaces. These projects are directed by logical exploration to guarantee hereditary manageability.

III. Logical Exploration Open doors

1. **Conduct Studies and Ethology**
   Hostage kangaroo conditions give controlled settings to top to bottom conduct studies and ethological research. Noticing social designs, correspondence examples, and regular ways of behaving inside hostage populaces adds to an exhaustive comprehension of kangaroo ethology. Such experiences illuminate both hostage the board rehearses and more extensive preservation methodologies.
2. **Conceptive Physiology and Wellbeing Exploration**
   Hostage kangaroo populaces offer open doors for definite examination into regenerative physiology and wellbeing. Concentrates on conceptive cycles, rearing ways of behaving, and wellbeing observing give significant information to the advancement of powerful rearing projects, veterinary consideration, and regenerative administration, helping both hostage and wild populaces.
3. **Dietary and Wholesome Examinations**

Painstakingly controlled slims down in hostage conditions consider exact dietary and healthful examinations. Understanding the nourishing prerequisites of kangaroos is fundamental for creating ideal taking care of practices in bondage. This information not just backings the wellbeing and prosperity of hostage people yet in addition illuminates natural surroundings the board techniques in nature.

IV. Instructive Jobs and Public Mindfulness

1. **Zoological Foundations as Instructive Centers**
   Zoological foundations lodging hostage kangaroos act as instructive centers, drawing in general society in vivid growth opportunities. Instructive projects, directed visits, and interpretive showcases give guests experiences into kangaroo science, conduct, and protection challenges. These establishments assume a urgent part in encouraging an association between people in general and natural life.
2. **Protection Informing and Support**
   Hostage kangaroo programs act as stages for protection informing and support. By displaying the difficulties looked by kangaroos in the wild, zoos and natural life safe-havens bring issues to light about the significance of territory protection, economical practices, and the job of people in worldwide preservation endeavors.
3. **School Projects and Effort**

Instructive effort reaches out past zoological establishments to incorporate school projects, studios, and local area outreach drives. Hostage kangaroos become ministers for their species, moving a feeling of obligation and sympathy in the more youthful age. Intuitive instructive projects give valuable open doors to understudies to find out about biodiversity, environment, and the interconnectedness of biological systems.

V. Challenges in Hostage Kangaroo The board

1. **Space Impediments and Walled in area Plan**
   One of the essential difficulties in hostage kangaroo the executives is tending to space limits and planning nooks that imitate normal environments. Adjusting the requirement for space with the limitations of bondage requires imaginative walled in area plan and the board methodologies to guarantee the physical and mental prosperity of the kangaroos.

2. **Social Variations to Imprisonment**
   Kangaroos might show conduct transformations to imprisonment, remembering changes for social elements and modified regenerative ways of behaving. Cautious checking and research are fundamental to comprehend and address these transformations, guaranteeing that hostage conditions support normal ways of behaving and social designs.

3. **Wellbeing and Government assistance Concerns**

Keeping up with the wellbeing and government assistance of hostage kangaroos includes tending to veterinary consideration, sustenance, and mental prosperity. Wellbeing challenges, for example, outer muscle issues or stress-related ways of behaving, require continuous checking and versatile administration techniques to upgrade the general personal satisfaction for hostage people.

VI. Advancements in Hostage Kangaroo The board

1. **Advancement Systems for Prosperity**
   Inventive enhancement methodologies, including physical, mental, and social advancement, are ceaselessly developing to address the different requirements of hostage kangaroos. From intuitive taking care of gadgets to computer generated reality reenactments, these systems expect to upgrade the general prosperity of kangaroos in imprisonment and advance normal ways of behaving.

2. **Innovative Reconciliation for Checking**
   Headways in innovation, for example, sensor-based frameworks and GPS beacons, work with constant checking of kangaroo conduct, wellbeing boundaries, and natural associations. Coordinating innovation into hostage the board rehearses considers more educated direction and exact changes in accordance with care conventions.

3. **Cooperative Exploration Drives**

Coordinated effort among zoological foundations, research associations, and preservation organizations upgrades the effect of hostage kangaroo the board. Joint exploration drives, information sharing organizations, and cooperative endeavors add to a more complete comprehension of kangaroo science and protection, cultivating an aggregate way to deal with natural life the board.

VII. Future Bearings and Supportability

1. **Territory Preservation and Rebuilding**

   The drawn out manageability of hostage kangaroo the board lies in equal endeavors to monitor and reestablish regular natural surroundings. Preservation associations and hostage the executives offices can team up on territory rebuilding projects, addressing the main drivers of dangers to kangaroo populaces in nature.

2. **Local area Commitment and Native Associations**

   Integrating people group commitment and cooperating with Native people group add to comprehensive preservation draws near. Native information and practices are priceless in figuring out kangaroo environment and social importance. Cooperative endeavors encourage a feeling of shared liability regarding the prosperity of kangaroo populaces.

3. **Instruction for Manageable Practices**

Instructive projects related with hostage kangaroo the executives can grow their concentration to incorporate feasible practices and capable untamed life stewardship. Empowering guests and the more extensive public to take on practical ways of behaving, support protection drives, and participate in moral natural life the travel industry adds to the more extensive objectives of biodiversity safeguarding.

5.1 Captive Kangaroos as Ambassadors for Wildlife Conservation

Hostage kangaroos, dwelling in zoological organizations and untamed life safehavens, expect an imperative job as diplomats for natural life protection. Past filling in as enthralling attractions for guests, these marsupials have a critical impact in bringing issues to light, cultivating an association between general society and untamed life, and adding to more extensive preservation drives. This investigation digs into the diverse jobs of hostage kangaroos as representatives, inspecting their effect on state funded instruction, protection informing, and the conservation of biodiversity.

II. The Meaning of Hostage Kangaroos

1. **Hereditary Repositories**

   Hostage kangaroos capability as hereditary repositories, defending the variety of their species. With some kangaroo populaces confronting dangers in the wild, including territory misfortune and environmental change, hostage people address a critical shield against the likely loss of remarkable hereditary characteristics.

2. **Protection Rearing Projects**

   Hostage kangaroos add to protection rearing projects focused on the recuperation of imperiled species. Via cautiously overseeing rearing, hereditary variety, and conceptive wellbeing, these projects support the objective of once again introducing practical populaces into their regular environments, at last adding to species preservation.

3. Social Exploration and Understanding

Noticing kangaroo conduct in bondage furnishes scientists with important bits of knowledge into their social designs, correspondence examples, and in general prosperity. Social examination upgrades how we might interpret kangaroos, adding to further developed hostage the executives practices and illuminating protection methodologies for their wild partners.

III. Protection Instruction through Hostage Kangaroos

1. Public Commitment and Association

Hostage kangaroos act as strong impetuses for public commitment, catching the consideration and interest of guests. Their charming presence cultivates an association between general society and natural life, rousing a feeling of miracle and interest. This close to home association shapes the reason for powerful preservation schooling.

2. Instructive Projects and Interpretive Presentations

Zoological establishments and untamed life asylums offer instructive projects and interpretive presentations revolved around hostage kangaroos. Directed visits, introductions, and intuitive displays furnish guests with data about kangaroo science, conduct, protection challenges, and the significance of biodiversity conservation.

3. School Projects and Effort Drives

Hostage kangaroos broaden their instructive effect past the bounds of zoos through school projects and local area outreach drives. Instructive effort programs bring preservation messages to schools, local area occasions, and online stages, contacting a different crowd and ingraining a feeling of obligation for natural life protection.

IV. Protection Informing and Promotion

1. Bringing issues to light about Dangers

Hostage kangaroos become diplomats for their species by bringing issues to light about the dangers looked by kangaroos in nature. Preservation informing stresses the effect of territory misfortune, environmental change, and human-untamed life struggle on kangaroo populaces, asking people to think about the more extensive ramifications for biodiversity.

2. Featuring Preservation Examples of overcoming adversity

Preservation examples of overcoming adversity, including those subsequent from hostage reproducing programs, act as incredible assets for promotion.

Hostage kangaroos that add to fruitful renewed introduction endeavors become living instances of the positive effect of preservation drives, moving expectation and empowering support for continuous endeavors.

3. **Empowering Reasonable Practices**

Preservation informing related with hostage kangaroos frequently stretches out to empowering feasible practices. Guests are taught about the significance of economical living, moral untamed life the travel industry, and capable decisions that add to the prosperity of kangaroos and their biological systems.

V. Challenges in Advancing Preservation through Hostage Kangaroos

1. **Adjusting Preservation and Government assistance**
   A key test is finding some kind of harmony between preservation goals and the government assistance of hostage kangaroos. Moral contemplations should guarantee that the prosperity and normal ways of behaving of people are focused on while as yet contributing definitively to protection objectives.

2. **Tending to Confusions and Generalizations**
   Hostage kangaroos additionally face the test of dissipating misguided judgments and generalizations. Certain social and media portrayals might sustain erroneous thoughts about kangaroos, and preservation informing should address and address these misinterpretations to encourage a more profound comprehension.

3. **Public Discernment and Commitment**

Guaranteeing supported public commitment represents a test, as starting interest in hostage kangaroos might wind down after some time. Creating inventive and continuous instructive projects, integrating new data, and making dynamic displays are fundamental to keeping up with public interest and inclusion.

VI. Inventive Ways to deal with Protection Schooling

1. **Intelligent Advancements and Virtual Stages**
   Inventive methodologies include utilizing intuitive advancements and virtual stages to improve the instructive experience. Computer generated reality reproductions, online instructive modules, and intuitive applications furnish guests with vivid experiences into kangaroo protection, supplementing customary on location shows.

2. **Cooperative Media Missions**
   Cooperative media crusades that highlight hostage kangaroos as diplomats can broaden the range of preservation messages. Cooperating with powerhouses, content makers, and natural life advocates enhances the effect of instructive substance, contacting assorted crowds through different internet based stages.

3. **Consolidating Native Information and Viewpoints**

Recognizing and consolidating Native information and viewpoints on kangaroos upgrades the realness and social pertinence of preservation schooling. Teaming up with Native people group guarantees that protection informing lines up with customary natural information and cultivates a more all encompassing way to deal with untamed life conservation.

VII. Future Headings and Supportability

1. **Local area Contribution in Preservation Projects**

   The future maintainability of involving hostage kangaroos as ministers for natural life protection lies in expanded local area contribution. Drawing in neighborhood networks in protection programs, consolidating their points of view, and encouraging a feeling of shared liability regarding kangaroo prosperity add to economical preservation endeavors.

2. **Research on the Effect of Instruction Projects**

   Continuous examination on the effect of training programs related with hostage kangaroos is vital. Surveying the adequacy of preservation informing, grasping guest discernments, and assessing conduct change coming about because of instructive drives illuminate persistent enhancements in protection training methodologies.

3. **Support for Worldwide Protection Drives**

Hostage kangaroos can assume a part in upholding for more extensive worldwide preservation drives. Zoological foundations and untamed life safe-havens can effectively partake in and support worldwide coordinated efforts, adding to the turn of events and execution of protection procedures on a worldwide scale.

5.2 Educational Programs and Outreach

Instructive projects and effort drives are indispensable parts of untamed life protection, offering a scaffold between general society and the normal world. In this investigation, we dive into the meaning of instructive projects and effort endeavors, with an emphasis on their part in encouraging ecological mindfulness, advancing feasible practices, and imparting a feeling of obligation towards biodiversity protection.

II. The Significance of Ecological Instruction

1. **Building Natural Proficiency**

   Instructive projects are crucial in building ecological education, outfitting people with information about biological systems, biodiversity, and the relationship of life on The planet. Ecological training enables individuals to settle on informed choices and make moves that add to the prosperity of the planet.

2. **Associating Individuals to Nature**

   Instructive drives assume an essential part in associating individuals to nature. By giving chances to coordinate encounters, nature strolls, and intelligent learning, people foster a more profound appreciation for the normal world. This association cultivates a feeling of obligation and stewardship towards the climate.

3. **Engaging People in the future**

Putting resources into natural training engages people in the future to turn out to be ecologically cognizant residents. Through instructive projects, youthful personalities gain the information and abilities expected to address natural difficulties, advocate for reasonable practices, and effectively partake in preservation endeavors.

III. Untamed life Preservation and Schooling

1. **Protection Through Mindfulness**
   Instructive projects act as useful assets for bringing issues to light about natural life protection. By featuring the significance of saving biodiversity, the difficulties looked by imperiled species, and the effect of human exercises on biological systems, these projects add to a more extensive comprehension of protection issues.

2. **Motivating Protection Activity**
   Past mindfulness, schooling rouses protection activity. Finding out about the situation of imperiled species, territory annihilation, and the results of environmental change persuades people to make strides towards positive change. Instructive drives give a pathway to transforming mindfulness into unmistakable protection endeavors.

3. **The Job of Zoos and Natural life Safe-havens**

Zoos and untamed life safe-havens assume a crucial part in untamed life protection schooling. Through on location instructive projects, directed visits, and intelligent displays, these organizations offer a one of a kind chance for the general population to interface with natural life, find out about preservation difficulties, and witness the positive effect of hostage reproducing and renewed introduction programs.

IV. Components of Viable Instructive Projects

1. **Connecting with Content and Intelligent Learning**
   Viable instructive projects integrate drawing in satisfied and intuitive growth opportunities. Using mixed media, involved exercises, and innovation upgrades the growing experience, making it more important and significant. Intelligent components catch the crowd's consideration and encourage a more profound comprehension of preservation ideas.

2. **Fitting Projects to Assorted Crowds**
   Perceiving the variety of crowds is fundamental for the outcome of instructive projects. Fitting substance to various age gatherings, social foundations, and

learning inclinations guarantees that the message resounds with a large number of people. Inclusivity advances openness and pertinence in instructive effort.

3. **True Associations and Contextual analyses**

Making true associations through contextual analyses and examples of overcoming adversity fortifies the effect of instructive projects. Displaying substantial instances of protection endeavors, local area drives, and positive results makes a story that moves people to trust in their ability to have an effect.

V. Outreach Drives: Broadening the Span

1. **Local area Commitment and Associations**
   Outreach drives include effectively captivating networks and shaping associations with nearby associations. Cooperative endeavors intensify the effect of instructive projects, contacting assorted crowds and utilizing the exceptional qualities of local area organizations.

2. **School Projects and Educational plan Mix**
   Bringing protection instruction into schools is an essential way to deal with arrive at youthful personalities. Coordinating ecological subjects into school educational programs, sorting out field excursions to nature saves, and giving assets to educators upgrade the instructive experience and make an enduring effect on understudies.

3. **Online Stages and Advanced Effort**

In the computerized age, online stages offer a unique road for outreach. Instructive substance, online classes, and virtual encounters contact a worldwide crowd, separating topographical hindrances. Virtual entertainment, instructive sites, and intelligent applications give available and drawing in stages to spreading preservation data.

VI. Examples of overcoming adversity in Protection Training

1. **Resident Science Drives**
   Resident science drives represent the progress of protection schooling. By including general society in logical exploration projects, these drives transform people into dynamic supporters of biodiversity observing, information assortment, and environmental examination, encouraging a feeling of pride and commitment.

2. **Local area drove Preservation Ventures**
   Local area drove preservation projects exhibit the force of limited endeavors. Engaging people group to assume responsibility for preservation drives, whether through natural surroundings rebuilding, untamed life observing, or supportable asset the board, makes a feeling of obligation and a more profound association with the climate.

3. Youth-drove Ecological Developments

Youth-drove ecological developments, driven by enthusiastic supporters, feature the extraordinary effect of training. Drives, for example, environment strikes, tree establishing efforts, and promotion for feasible practices outline how educated and spurred youth can drive positive change and impact more extensive cultural perspectives.

VII. Challenges In Preservation Training and Effort

1. Conquering Ecological Lack of concern

A huge test in preservation schooling is defeating ecological lack of care. Now and again, people might feel detached from ecological issues or see them as far off and inconsequential to their regular routines. Fitting instructive projects to address this lack of care requires innovative methodologies that underline individual pertinence and interconnectedness.

2. Exploring Social Contrasts

Social contrasts can present difficulties in planning generally successful instructive projects. Understanding and regarding assorted social viewpoints is fundamental to guarantee that protection messages are gotten decidedly and resound with various networks.

3. Tending to Data Over-burden

In the period of data, tending to data over-burden is a test. Instructive projects should work out some kind of harmony between giving extensive data and trying not to overpower crowds. Zeroed in, clear informing that focuses on key protection ideas is significant for powerful correspondence.

VIII. Developments in Preservation Training

1. Increased Reality and Augmented Reality Encounters

Integrating increased reality (AR) and augmented reality (VR) encounters into instructive projects offers creative ways of drawing in crowds. Virtual voyages through biological systems, intuitive untamed life experiences, and vivid learning conditions upgrade the instructive experience and catch the creative mind of members.

2. Gamification of Preservation Learning

Gamification includes coordinating game components into instructive substance to make learning more intelligent and agreeable. Preservation themed games, tests, and difficulties transform instruction into a lively and compensating experience, empowering dynamic support and information maintenance.

3. Intelligent Portable Applications and Digital broadcasts

Portable applications and digital recordings give available stages to in a hurry protection learning. Intelligent applications with tests, virtual field guides, and continuous reports on protection projects keep clients locked in. Webcasts highlighting master interviews, narrating, and conversations make complex protection points more receptive.

IX. Future Headings in Protection Schooling

1. **Environmental Change Schooling**

   The criticalness of environmental change highlights the requirement for devoted environmental change instruction. Future preservation schooling projects ought to focus on environment proficiency, assisting people with figuring out the causes, effects, and answers for environmental change, and enabling them to add to relief and transformation endeavors.

2. **Incorporation of Native Information**

   Recognizing and consolidating Native information in protection schooling is a developing need. Future projects ought to effectively look for Native viewpoints on ecological stewardship, biodiversity preservation, and maintainable works on, encouraging a more comprehensive and socially delicate methodology.

3. **Worldwide Cooperation and Information Sharing**

The fate of preservation training lies in worldwide cooperation and information sharing. Laying out networks that work with the trading of best practices, examples of overcoming adversity, and imaginative methodologies guarantees that protection training stays dynamic, informed by assorted encounters, and receptive to arising difficulties.

5.3 Research Opportunities in Captive Environments

Hostage conditions offer extraordinary examination valuable open doors that contribute fundamentally to how we might interpret untamed life science, conduct, and preservation. This investigation digs into the assorted examination roads accessible inside hostage settings, accentuating their importance to species the executives, living space safeguarding, and the more extensive field of protection science.

1. **Social Investigations and Ethology**

   Hostage conditions give controlled settings helpful for top to bottom social examinations and ethological research. Noticing the way of behaving of creatures, for example, kangaroos, in bondage permits specialists to investigate social designs, correspondence examples, and reactions to ecological boosts. The controlled circumstances empower a degree of detail and accuracy that might be trying to accomplish in nature.

   Model: Grasping Social Elements

   Scientists can examine the arrangement of social orders, mating ways of behaving, and bunch connections among hostage kangaroos. This information contributes not exclusively to the prosperity of people in imprisonment yet in addition illuminates preservation systems in the wild by explaining basic parts of social elements.

2. **Regenerative Physiology and Wellbeing Exploration**

   Hostage populaces offer an interesting an open door to lead nitty gritty examination on regenerative physiology and wellbeing. Concentrating on regenerative cycles, rearing ways of behaving, and in general wellbeing in controlled conditions gives important bits of knowledge that can be applied to upgrade rearing projects, address conceptive difficulties, and add to the general prosperity of the species.

   Model: Exploring Conceptive Wellbeing

   Analysts can screen the conceptive strength of hostage kangaroos, concentrating on variables like hormonal examples, mating ways of behaving, and pregnancy results.

   This exploration not just guides in that frame of mind of hostage populaces yet in addition illuminates more extensive preservation endeavors by giving information on conceptive physiology.

3. **Dietary and Healthful Investigations**

   Controlled abstains from food in hostage conditions consider exact dietary and wholesome examinations. Grasping the wholesome prerequisites of creatures, including kangaroos, adds to the advancement of ideal taking care of practices in bondage. This information is significant for keeping up with the wellbeing and prosperity of hostage people and can likewise illuminate natural surroundings the board methodologies in nature.

   Model: Streamlining Diets

   Specialists can explore the effect of various eating regimens on the wellbeing, proliferation, and life span of hostage kangaroos. This data refines dietary rules for hostage the executives, guaranteeing that nourishing necessities are met and possibly offering bits of knowledge into searching propensities in nature.

4. **Veterinary Consideration and Wellbeing Observing**

   Hostage conditions work with standard wellbeing checks and observing, offering an abundance of information for veterinary exploration. Scientists can concentrate on the commonness of medical problems, reactions to clinical intercessions, and the general wellbeing patterns of hostage populaces. This examination is indispensable for preventive consideration and the advancement of compelling wellbeing the board conventions.

   Model: Wellbeing Observing

   Through nonstop wellbeing observing, specialists can recognize examples of sicknesses, stress-related ways of behaving, and other wellbeing pointers among hostage kangaroos. This data guides veterinary mediations, adds to the prosperity of people in bondage, and illuminates more extensive wellbeing methodologies for wild populaces.

5. **Mental and Social Improvement**

Concentrating on the mental capacities of creatures in imprisonment is an arising research region with suggestions for their general prosperity. Mental advancement, including exercises that invigorate mental cycles, permits scientists to investigate the insight, critical thinking abilities, and versatility of hostage people.

Model: Mental Enhancement Studies

Specialists can configuration analyses to evaluate the mental capacities of kangaroos, for example, their critical thinking abilities, memory, and capacity to adjust to new difficulties. Understanding mental cycles adds to the advancement of viable enhancement methodologies, upgrading the psychological prosperity of hostage people.

6. **Social Construction and Elements**

The investigation of social designs and elements inside hostage populaces gives important experiences into the social way of behaving of species. Hostage conditions permit specialists to control social groupings, notice associations, and investigate the effect of social elements on individual prosperity.

Model: Social Design Examinations

Analysts can direct examinations to control gathering creations among hostage kangaroos, seeing what changes in collective vibes mean for social connections, feelings of anxiety, and by and large way of behaving. This data illuminates hostage the board rehearses and adds to how we might interpret the social designs of kangaroo populaces.

7. **Preservation Hereditary qualities**

Hostage conditions act as stores of hereditary variety, offering open doors for protection hereditary qualities research. Concentrating on the hereditary cosmetics of hostage populaces recognizes one of a kind hereditary qualities, evaluate the soundness of the genetic stock, and add to educated reproducing techniques for the preservation regarding species.

Model: Hereditary Variety Investigation

Specialists can direct hereditary investigations on hostage kangaroo populaces to survey levels of variety, distinguish likely hereditary bottlenecks, and illuminate reproducing programs pointed toward keeping a sound and hereditarily strong populace. This examination has suggestions for the protection of hereditary variety in both hostage and wild settings.

8. **Similar Examinations Among Hostage and Wild Populaces**

Near investigations among hostage and wild populaces give significant experiences into the effect of imprisonment on the way of behaving, physiology, and generally prosperity of creatures. Understanding the similitudes and contrasts among hostage and out of control people adds to more compelling hostage the executives and illuminates preservation methodologies.

Model: Stress Reactions in Imprisonment

Scientists can look at pressure reactions among hostage and wild kangaroo populaces, concentrating on physiological signs of pressure. This exploration recognizes likely stressors in hostage conditions and guides the advancement of the executives rehearses that advance the mental prosperity of people.

Chapter 6

Legal And Ethical Considerations

Hostage natural life the executives includes a perplexing interchange of lawful, moral, and protection contemplations. Adjusting the government assistance of individual creatures, protection objectives, and public interests requires an exhaustive comprehension of the legitimate and moral structures overseeing hostage conditions. In this investigation, we dig into the multi-layered elements of legitimate and moral contemplations in hostage untamed life the executives, analyzing the administrative scene, moral standards, and the advancing elements of human-creature connections.

II. The Administrative Scene

1. **Peaceful accords and Shows**

   Hostage untamed life the board is dependent upon peaceful accords and shows pointed toward rationing biodiversity and guaranteeing moral treatment. Shows, for example, the Show on Worldwide Exchange Jeopardized Types of Wild Fauna and Verdure (Refers to) set rules for the global exchange of untamed life, including arrangements for hostage reproducing and preservation programs.

2. **Public Regulation and Guidelines**

   Every nation has its own arrangement of regulations and guidelines overseeing hostage natural life. These legitimate structures address issues like licenses for hostage reproducing, transportation of creatures, and principles for the consideration and lodging of hostage species. Public regulation frequently mirrors a country's obligation to biodiversity preservation and creature government assistance.

3. **Zoo and Untamed life Guidelines**

Explicit guidelines relating to zoos, untamed life safe-havens, and other hostage offices exist to guarantee the moral and sympathetic treatment of creatures. These guidelines might cover nook plan, veterinary consideration, rearing projects, and public security. Zoos, specifically, are much of the time subject to authorization guidelines set by industry associations.

III. Moral Standards in Hostage Untamed life The board

1. **Creature Government assistance and Prosperity**
   Guaranteeing the government assistance and prosperity of hostage creatures is a crucial moral thought. Moral standards direct that creatures ought to be given conditions that meet their physiological and conduct needs, admittance to fitting veterinary consideration, and open doors for regular ways of behaving. The Five Opportunities system — independence from yearning and thirst, independence from uneasiness, independence from agony, injury, or illness, opportunity to communicate typical way of behaving, and independence from dread and misery — guides moral contemplations in hostage settings.

2. **Preservation Morals**
   Hostage natural life the executives is frequently determined by protection morals, underscoring the job of hostage reproducing programs in species preservation. Moral contemplations incorporate keeping up with hereditary variety, forestalling the elimination of imperiled species, and adding to renewed introduction endeavors. Whether or unsure species ought to be saved in imprisonment for protection designs involves progressing moral discussion.

3. **Instructive and Exploration Morals**

Hostage conditions are frequently used for instructive and research purposes. Moral contemplations in these settings include guaranteeing that instructive projects are exact, conscious, and add to preservation mindfulness. Research led in bondage should comply with moral rules, including getting educated assent (where appropriate), limiting mischief to creatures, and leading examinations with logical legitimacy.

IV. Challenges in Legitimate and Moral Consistence

1. **Authorization and Checking**
   One of the difficulties in the lawful and moral scene of hostage natural life the executives is the implementation and observing of guidelines. Irregularities in implementation across districts or careless checking systems can prompt infringement of moral guidelines and legitimate necessities.

2. **Understanding of Moral Standards**
   The understanding of moral standards can change among partners, including creature government assistance promoters, moderates, and office administrators. Conflicts might emerge in regards to what comprises suitable consideration, preservation needs, or the moral legitimizations for keeping specific species in imprisonment.

3. **Arising Moral Issues**

Headways in logical information, changing cultural mentalities, and developing points of view on basic entitlements lead to arising moral issues. Discusses encompassing the morals of quality altering, cloning, and the utilization of creatures in diversion challenge conventional standards and require nonstop reassessment of moral structures.

V. Advancing Viewpoints on Human-Creature Connections

1. **Shift Toward Moral Contemplations**
   By and large, the treatment of hostage creatures was basically seen from the perspective of diversion or protection without continuously giving due thought to moral worries. Lately, there has been a critical shift toward integrating moral contemplations into the administration of hostage natural life, reflecting developing cultural mentalities toward creatures.

2. **Public Discernment and Promotion**
   Public discernment assumes a vital part in molding legitimate and moral guidelines for hostage untamed life the board. Expanded public mindfulness, filled by backing efforts and admittance to data, has prompted uplifted assumptions for the moral treatment of creatures in imprisonment. Zoos and different offices are presently under expanded examination with respect to their practices.

3. **Changing Perspectives toward Imprisonment**

Society's perspectives toward the imprisonment of creatures have developed, prompting a more prominent accentuation on establishing conditions that focus on creature government assistance. This shift is apparent in the developing notoriety of asylums, which center around giving lifetime care to creatures resigned from bazaars, the outlandish pet exchange, and different circumstances, underscoring their prosperity over diversion.

VI. Contextual analyses: Legitimate and Moral Difficulties

1. **The Tiger Lord Debate**
   The narrative series "Tiger Lord" focused on the moral and legitimate difficulties related with private responsibility for felines in the US. The case featured issues of rearing, protection claims, and the absence of predictable government guidelines overseeing the keeping of fascinating creatures in imprisonment.

2. **Orca Imprisonment and Amusement**

The utilization of orcas in marine parks for diversion purposes has been a point of convergence of lawful and moral discussions. Narratives like "Blackfish" shed light on the effect of imprisonment on orcas' prosperity, starting expanded examination of marine well evolved creature stops and calls for stricter guidelines.

VII. Developments in Moral Untamed life The executives

1. **Progressions in Nook Plan**
   Developments in nook configuration center around establishing conditions that focus on the mental and actual prosperity of hostage creatures. Bigger, more naturalistic nooks with highlights like climbing structures, water elements, and advancement exercises add to the moral treatment of creatures.

2. **Social and Mental Advancement**
   Moral natural life the executives stresses the significance of giving conduct and mental advancement to hostage creatures. Techniques like riddle feeders, instructional meetings, and intelligent exercises upgrade the psychological feeling of creatures, lessening pressure and advancing normal ways of behaving.

3. **Protection centered Coordinated efforts**

Moral contemplations in hostage untamed life the board stretch out to cooperative endeavors among offices, preservation associations, and scientists. Key associations work with the sharing of information, hereditary material, and best works on, adding to more powerful protection results.

VIII. Future Bearings in Legitimate and Moral Untamed life The executives

1. **Worldwide Guidelines for Hostage Natural life Government assistance**
   The fate of lawful and moral untamed life the board might include the improvement of worldwide principles for the government assistance of hostage creatures. Cooperative endeavors among nations, global associations, and partners can prompt the foundation of moral rules material across borders.

2. **Improved Straightforwardness and Responsibility**
   Expanding straightforwardness and responsibility in hostage natural life the board is probably going to be a focal point of future turns of events. Offices might be supposed to give more definite data about their practices, care principles, and protection commitments to measure up to the assumptions of an educated and honest public.

3. **Regulation Tending to Arising Innovations**

As arising innovations, for example, quality altering and cloning, become more predominant, lawful and moral systems might have to adjust to address the ramifications for hostage untamed life. Regulation and rules will probably develop to explore the moral difficulties presented by these innovations.

6.1 International and National Regulations

Hostage untamed life the executives is a perplexing field that includes the consideration, protection, and moral treatment of creatures in controlled conditions. To guarantee the government assistance of hostage untamed life and address protection targets, both worldwide and public guidelines assume a significant part. This investigation analyzes the different administrative structures overseeing hostage untamed life the board, zeroing in on peaceful accords, public regulation, and the difficulties and amazing open doors inborn in the crossing point of legitimate and moral contemplations.

II. Peaceful accords and Shows

1. **Show on Worldwide Exchange Imperiled Types of Wild Fauna and Vegetation (Refers to)**

   Refers to is a foundation peaceful accord pointed toward directing the global exchange of untamed life. The show, took on in 1973, assumes a vital part in guaranteeing that the exchange wild creatures and plants doesn't undermine their endurance. Refers to records species in Supplements I, II, and III, each conveying various degrees of security and exchange limitations. For hostage untamed life the board, Refers to is especially pertinent in controlling the cross-line development of jeopardized species, incorporating those saved in imprisonment for protection purposes.

2. **The World Relationship of Zoos and Aquariums (WAZA)**

   WAZA is a worldwide partnership of territorial and public relationship of zoos and aquariums. While not an administrative body, WAZA gives rules and principles to its part establishments. These rules cover perspectives like creature government assistance, protection endeavors, and moral contemplations in hostage settings. Part zoos and aquariums are supposed to stick to these guidelines, adding to the general harmonization of practices in hostage untamed life the board on a global scale.

3. **Bonn Show (CMS) - Protection of Transitory Types of Wild Creatures**

The Bonn Show, otherwise called the CMS (Show on the Preservation of Transitory Types of Wild Creatures), centers around the protection of transient species and their environments.

Albeit not solely designated at hostage untamed life, CMS perceives the significance of saving species all through their transitory reach, which incorporates both wild and hostage conditions. The show urges worldwide participation to address dangers to transitory species, incorporating those looked in bondage.

III. Public Regulation and Guidelines

1. **US: Creature Government assistance Act (AWA)**

   In the US, the Creature Government assistance Act (AWA) is a bureaucratic regulation that sets guidelines for the treatment of creatures in research, presentation, transport, and by vendors. The AWA is controlled by the US Division of Horticulture (USDA) and remembers arrangements well defined for creatures for imprisonment, like those in zoos, carnivals, and examination offices. The

AWA frames prerequisites for lodging, dealing with, veterinary consideration, and transportation of hostage creatures.

2. **Joined Realm: Zoo Authorizing Act**

The Assembled Realm's Zoo Authorizing Act controls the activity of zoos, guaranteeing the prosperity of creatures kept in bondage. Under this regulation, zoos are expected to get a permit to work, and the authorizing system includes evaluations of creature government assistance, protection commitments, and schooling programs. The Demonstration means to find some kind of harmony between the public's happiness regarding zoo visits and the moral treatment of creatures.

3. **Australia: Climate Security and Biodiversity Preservation Act (EPBC Act)**

Australia's EPBC Act is a thorough piece of regulation tending to natural insurance and protection, including hostage untamed life the board. The Demonstration covers the import and product of natural life, as well as the protection of compromised species. It requires grants for specific exercises including local natural life and layouts standards for the moral treatment and protection of Australia's interesting fauna.

IV. Difficulties and Potential open doors in Consistence

1. **Harmonization of Principles**

One of the difficulties in hostage untamed life the executives is accomplishing harmonization of guidelines across global and public levels. Unique guidelines and requirement components can make irregularities in how hostage offices work and may prompt varieties in creature government assistance and preservation results. Endeavors toward adjusting norms and advancing worldwide participation are fundamental to tending to this test.

2. **Authorization and Checking**

Implementing and checking consistence with guidelines present critical difficulties. A few locales might come up short on assets or foundation to screen hostage offices, prompting expected infringement of norms really. Fortifying requirement systems and elevating straightforwardness are vital for address issues connected with rebelliousness.

3. **Arising Moral and Logical Contemplations**

As logical comprehension and moral contemplations in hostage untamed life the board develop, guidelines should adjust to resolve arising issues. Banters around the utilization of arising innovations, quality altering, and cloning feature the requirement for administrative systems that record for moral and logical progressions while guaranteeing the government assistance of hostage creatures.

V. Moral Contemplations in Administrative Consistence

1. **Creature Government assistance and Protection Morals**

   Administrative consistence ought to line up with moral standards enveloping creature government assistance and preservation needs. Moral contemplations incorporate giving conditions that meet the conduct and physiological necessities of creatures, adding to protection endeavors, and advancing the moral treatment of hostage untamed life in accordance with developing cultural perspectives.

2. **Straightforwardness and Public Trust**

   Moral contemplations in administrative consistence stretch out to straightforwardness and public trust. Open correspondence about the circumstances in which creatures are kept, preservation commitments, and adherence to moral rules fabricates public trust. Straightforwardness cultivates responsibility and permits people in general to come to informed conclusions about supporting hostage offices.

3. **Adjusting Preservation and Creature Government assistance**

A huge moral test is finding some kind of harmony between preservation objectives and individual creature government assistance. Some preservation reproducing programs include saving creatures in imprisonment for expanded periods, bringing up moral issues about the drawn out prosperity of people. Guidelines ought to explore this fragile equilibrium, guaranteeing that preservation endeavors don't think twice about government assistance of the creatures in question.

VI. Advancements in Administrative Methodologies

1. **Result based Guidelines**

   Inventive ways to deal with guidelines include advancing toward result based principles as opposed to prescriptive measures. This shift centers around assessing the consequences of hostage natural life the board rehearses, for example, the general prosperity of creatures and the outcome of protection programs. Result based guidelines give adaptability while guaranteeing wanted results.

2. **Innovation and Information driven Consistence**

   Headways in innovation, including checking frameworks, information examination, and man-made reasoning, offer open doors for more viable consistence observing. Innovation driven arrangements can improve information assortment, survey creature prosperity progressively, and work with more proficient requirement of guidelines, particularly in huge or far off offices.

3. **Worldwide Coordinated effort and Information Sharing**

Advancing worldwide coordinated effort and information sharing is an imaginative way to deal with address difficulties in administrative consistence. Laying out stages for nations, associations, and specialists to share best practices, research discoveries, and fruitful systems upgrades the aggregate capacity to further develop guidelines and encourage moral hostage natural life the executives.

VII. Future Bearings in Guideline and Consistence

1. **Worldwide Certificate Norms**

   The future might observer the advancement of global certificate guidelines for hostage natural life the executives. These principles, similar to those in different businesses, could give a worldwide perceived system to surveying consistence, guaranteeing moral treatment, and advancing prescribed procedures in hostage offices.

2. **Incorporation of Arising Advances**

   Administrative structures will probably have to incorporate arising innovations, like hereditary altering and high level checking frameworks. Proactive thought of the moral ramifications of these advancements, combined with administrative direction, will be fundamental to explore their mindful use in hostage natural life the board.

3. **Versatile Guidelines**

Given the powerful idea of the field, future guidelines ought to embrace flexibility. Versatile administrative structures can consolidate new logical discoveries, moral contemplations, and cultural assumptions. This adaptability permits guidelines to develop close by progressions in information and innovation.

6.2 Ethical Dilemmas in Keeping Kangaroos in Captivity

The keeping of kangaroos in imprisonment raises complex moral predicaments that entwine contemplations of creature government assistance, preservation objectives, and the developing viewpoints on human-creature connections. As notorious images of Australia's novel natural life, kangaroos enthrall the public's creative mind and are dependent upon different administration rehearses in zoos, safe-havens, and other hostage settings. This investigation dives into the moral situations encompassing the imprisonment of kangaroos, inspecting central points of contention, for example, government assistance concerns, protection morals, and the harmony between open commitment and individual prosperity.

II. Government assistance Concerns and Basic entitlements

1. **Physical and Mental Prosperity**

   One of the essential moral predicaments in keeping kangaroos in bondage spins around guaranteeing their physical and mental prosperity. Hostage conditions, even those planned with the best expectations, may battle to give the tremendous, normal living spaces and social designs fundamental for kangaroo well-being. Issues like restricted space, lacking advancement, and control can prompt pressure, conduct anomalies, and compromised prosperity.

2. **Opportunity of Development and Normal Ways of behaving**
   Kangaroos are eminent for their strong rear appendages, adjusted for jumping over significant distances. The moral inquiry emerges with regards to whether hostage settings can sufficiently meet the normal conduct needs of kangaroos, including bouncing, brushing, and mingling. The limitation of these natural ways of behaving in bondage raises worries about the creatures' opportunity of development and their capacity to communicate their species-explicit ways of behaving.

3. **Moral Contemplations of Repression**

The actual demonstration of binding kangaroos to walled in areas prompts moral contemplations. Pundits contend that saving creatures in bondage for human perception or amusement might encroach upon their characteristic right to live openly right at home. The moral test is to adjust the instructive and preservation advantages of hostage conditions with the honest conviction to regard the independence of individual creatures.

III. Preservation Morals and Hostage Rearing Projects

1. **Preservation Worth of Hostage Rearing**
   Hostage reproducing programs are in many cases legitimized by their expected commitments to species protection. Kangaroos, in the same way as other natural life species, face dangers like living space misfortune, illness, and environmental change. Hostage rearing plans to keep up with hereditary variety, make protection populaces, and, at times, work with renewed introduction into nature. The moral problem lies in deciding the degree to which bondage is morally legitimate for protection purposes.

2. **Long haul Imprisonment and Protection Results**
   A moral issue emerges while thinking about the drawn out bondage of kangaroos in rearing projects. While imprisonment might offer assurance from quick dangers, questions arise in regards to the creatures' personal satisfaction, expected loss of wild ways of behaving, and the adequacy of renewed introduction endeavors. The moral harmony between transient protection gains and potential long haul disservices stays a mind boggling thought.

3. **Uprightness of Regular Ways of behaving in Hostage Rearing**

Keeping up with the respectability of normal ways of behaving is critical in hostage rearing projects. Moral difficulties arise when bondage modifies ways of behaving basic to the endurance of the species in nature. For kangaroos, this might incorporate social designs, scavenging ways of behaving, and hunter evasion components. Finding some kind of harmony between hostage reproducing endeavors and saving normal ways of behaving represents a continuous moral predicament.

IV. Public Commitment and Schooling

1. **Instructive Worth of Hostage Kangaroos**
   Hostage kangaroos act as instructive envoys, furnishing the general population with a chance to find out about these notorious marsupials. The moral inquiry emerges with regards to whether the instructive advantages legitimize the imprisonment of kangaroos. Evaluating the instructive worth includes considering the precision of data introduced, the effect on open discernments, and the potential for moving preservation activity.

2. **Morals of Creature Showcases and Diversion**
   Zoos and natural life stops frequently highlight kangaroos in creature presentations, shows, or intuitive experiences to draw in guests. The moral predicament focuses on the line between instructive encounters and diversion. Questions emerge about whether such shows focus on the government assistance of the creatures or cater principally to human satisfaction, possibly compromising the moral respectability of imprisonment.

3. **Public Insight and Preservation Backing**

Public discernment assumes a critical part in the moral contemplations of keeping kangaroos in imprisonment. Positive encounters with hostage kangaroos can cultivate sympathy, bring issues to light about preservation challenges, and move support for natural life protection drives. In any case, negative encounters or view of lacking consideration can prompt public kickback and calls for worked on moral principles in hostage settings.

V. Moral Rules and Industry Norms

1. **WAZA and Moral Norms**
   The World Relationship of Zoos and Aquariums (WAZA) lays out moral rules for its part establishments, including those lodging kangaroos. These rules accentuate the government assistance of creatures, preservation endeavors, and training. Nonetheless, adherence to these principles shifts among offices, and the viability of such rules in tending to the moral predicaments of kangaroo imprisonment is dependent upon progressing examination.

2. **Public Regulation and Administrative Oversight**

Public regulation and administrative oversight assume a significant part in forming the moral scene of kangaroo imprisonment. Regulations overseeing the consideration, the executives, and display of natural life, for example, the Creature Government assistance Act in the US or comparable regulation in different nations, give a legitimate structure to moral contemplations. Notwithstanding, the adequacy of these guidelines in tending to explicit moral issues might change.

VI. Defeating Moral Difficulties

1. **Progressions in Fenced in area Plan and Farming**
   Developments in fenced in area plan and farming practices offer roads for tending to moral predicaments in kangaroo imprisonment. Bigger, more naturalistic nooks that impersonate the kangaroos' regular territory, combined with conduct and mental improvement, can upgrade the prosperity of hostage people. Consistent headways there add to moral enhancements in kangaroo the board.

2. **Research on Hostage Government assistance and Conduct**
   Logical examination zeroed in on the government assistance and conduct of hostage kangaroos gives significant experiences to tending to moral worries. Studies surveying pressure pointers, social elements, and the effect of bondage on kangaroo conduct add to confirm based rehearses that focus on the prosperity of creatures in imprisonment.

3. **Preservation centered Joint efforts**

Coordinated efforts between hostage offices, protection associations, and specialists can improve the moral groundworks of kangaroo imprisonment. Sharing information, partaking in protection drives, and adding to explore endeavors by and large help moral practices that line up with both the government assistance of individual kangaroos and more extensive preservation objectives.

6.3 Advocacy and Activism for Kangaroo Rights
Backing and activism for kangaroo privileges have picked up speed as a moral objective and a critical part of untamed life preservation endeavors. Kangaroos, notorious images of Australia's one of a kind fauna, face different difficulties, including territory misfortune, separating, and bondage. This investigation digs into the blossoming development pushing for kangaroo freedoms, analyzing the moral contemplations, preservation objectives, and the advancing scene of public mindfulness and activism encompassing these wonderful marsupials.

II. The Moral Goal

1. **Regarding Inborn Worth**
   Support for kangaroo privileges is established in the conviction that each person, paying little heed to species, has innate worth and the option to live liberated from superfluous damage. Moral contemplations underline the need to perceive the independence, normal ways of behaving, and prosperity of kangaroos in their local territories and imprisonment.

2. **Adjusting Preservation and Individual Government assistance**
   Moral promotion tries to figure out some kind of harmony between protection goals and the government assistance of individual kangaroos. While protection endeavors are fundamental for keeping up with biodiversity, moral

contemplations highlight the significance of guaranteeing that these endeavors don't think twice about prosperity of kangaroos, both in the wild and in imprisonment.

3. **Relieving Anthropogenic Dangers**

Advocates center around addressing anthropogenic dangers to kangaroos, including territory obliteration, vehicle crashes, and separating programs. Moral objectives call for proactive measures to moderate these dangers, safeguard kangaroo populaces, and advance agreeable concurrence among people and untamed life.

III. Protection Objectives

1. **Protecting Territory and Biodiversity**
   A focal fundamental of kangaroo freedoms support is the conservation of normal territories. Safeguarding the biological systems where kangaroos flourish is fundamental for keeping up with biodiversity, supporting local verdure, and shielding the sensitive equilibrium of Australia's extraordinary scenes.

2. **Elective Ways to deal with Populace The board**
   Advocates look for elective ways to deal with populace the executives that focus on non-deadly strategies. The accentuation is on utilizing moral, proof based methodologies to address human-natural life clashes, diminish negative associations, and investigate imaginative arrangements that regard the inborn worth of kangaroo lives.

3. **Supporting Maintainable Protection Practices**

Kangaroo privileges advocates champion reasonable preservation rehearses that focus on the drawn out prosperity of kangaroo populaces. This includes supporting examination on kangaroo nature, carrying out territory rebuilding drives, and advancing dependable land the executives rehearses.

IV. The Job of Public Mindfulness

1. **Moving Public Insights**
   Backing for kangaroo freedoms depends on moving public insights and encouraging sympathy towards these marsupials. Training and mindfulness crusades mean to dissipate legends, challenge misguided judgments, and give exact data about kangaroo conduct, environment, and their necessary job in Australia's biological systems.

2. **Featuring the Morals of Business Kangaroo Industry**
   The business kangaroo industry, which includes the collecting of kangaroo meat and stows away, is a point of convergence of moral examination. Advocates work to uncover the moral worries encompassing business reaping, including

issues connected with creature government assistance, biological manageability, and the effect on kangaroo populaces.

3. **Enabling General society to Backer**

Promotion endeavors engage people in general to become vocal advocates for kangaroo freedoms. Through missions, petitions, and grassroots drives, advocates urge people to voice their interests, draw in with policymakers, and effectively add to the moral treatment and preservation of kangaroos.

V. Legitimate Securities and Difficulties

1. **Existing Lawful Systems**
Backing for kangaroo privileges frequently converges with existing lawful systems. While certain districts have securities set up, for example, limitations on the business kangaroo industry, advocates make progress toward reinforcing and extending these legitimate protections. This incorporates upholding for additional thorough guidelines that address living space assurance, empathetic populace the executives, and moral contemplations in bondage.

2. **Challenges in Authorization**
Advocates face difficulties in the authorization of existing regulations and guidelines. Conflicting authorization, careless punishments for infringement, and holes in administrative oversight add to progressing moral worries. Reinforcing lawful components and tending to these difficulties are key goals for kangaroo freedoms advocates.

3. **Worldwide Cooperation for Lawful Insurances**

Given the transient idea of some kangaroo species, worldwide cooperation is fundamental. Advocates try to lay out peaceful accords and participation to guarantee the security of kangaroos across their reach. This includes sharing information, blending legitimate norms, and aggregately tending to transboundary protection challenges.

VI. Grassroots Activism and Drives

1. **Salvage and Restoration Endeavors**
Grassroots activism remembers hands-for drives like salvage and restoration endeavors for harmed or stranded kangaroos. Advocates work to make organizations of workers, natural life carers, and recovery focuses that give care and backing to kangaroos out of luck.

2. **Local area Drove Preservation Tasks**
Neighborhood people group assume a crucial part in kangaroo freedoms backing. Local area drove preservation projects, territory rebuilding drives, and resident science programs enable people to add to the assurance and moral treatment of kangaroos in their districts effectively.

3. **Advancing Moral The travel industry Practices**

Support stretches out to advancing moral the travel industry rehearses that regard kangaroos in their normal environments. This includes empowering capable natural life seeing, supporting eco-accommodating the travel industry administrators, and bringing issues to light about the likely effect of the travel industry on kangaroo conduct and living spaces.

VII. Difficulties and Reactions

1. **Financial Interests and Protection from Change**
   Support for kangaroo privileges faces difficulties from financial interests attached to the business kangaroo industry. Protection from change, established in monetary contemplations, presents obstacles for carrying out moral other options and progressing towards additional supportable and compassionate practices.
2. **Offsetting Preservation with Human Requirements**
   Pundits contend that some support endeavors might ignore the need to offset kangaroo protection with human requirements, particularly in locales where kangaroo populaces might affect farming or foundation. Finding some kind of harmony that regards both environmental uprightness and human livelihoods stays a mind boggling challenge.
3. **Exploring Social Viewpoints**

Promotion experiences difficulties in exploring assorted social points of view and mentalities towards kangaroos. Understanding and regarding Native viewpoints, nearby customs, and local varieties in human-untamed life connections are essential for powerful support that recognizes the social setting.

VIII. Future Headings in Kangaroo Freedoms Support

1. **Coordination of Native Information**
   The fate of kangaroo privileges support includes a more profound mix of Native information and points of view. Teaming up with Native people group, recognizing conventional environmental information, and consolidating Native voices in protection drives are fundamental for socially touchy and successful backing.
2. **Mechanical Advancements in Protection**
   Backing for kangaroo freedoms can profit from mechanical advancements. Propels in observing advancements, information examination, and remote detecting can improve protection endeavors, give bits of knowledge into kangaroo conduct, and add to confirm based navigation.
3. **Worldwide Systems administration and Cooperation**

Future bearings in kangaroo freedoms promotion incorporate fortifying worldwide systems administration and coordinated effort. Laying out worldwide partnerships, sharing prescribed procedures, and encouraging an aggregate obligation to moral treatment and preservation can intensify the effect of support endeavors.

Chapter 7

Future Directions

As we stand at the convergence of natural difficulties, developing moral points of view, and mechanical headways, the eventual fate of kangaroo preservation and the board is a dynamic and multi-layered scene. This investigation dives into the expected future headings for kangaroo protection, tending to key regions, for example, living space conservation, economical administration rehearses, progressions in innovation, local area commitment, and worldwide cooperation. By imagining and effectively molding the future, we can pursue guaranteeing the prosperity of kangaroo populaces, the conservation of their normal territories, and the agreeable conjunction of people and kangaroos.

II. Reasonable Natural surroundings Protection

1. **Development and Availability of Safeguarded Regions**
   The fate of kangaroo preservation relies on the development and availability of safeguarded regions. Endeavors to make and keep up with natural life passages that connection divided territories are essential. This approach works with quality stream, mitigates the effect of living space discontinuity, and improves the flexibility of kangaroo populaces notwithstanding ecological changes.

2. **Reclamation of Debased Environments**
   Putting resources into living space reclamation undertakings will be foremost before long. Reestablishing debased environments gives extra space to kangaroo populaces as well as adds to the general soundness of biological systems. Once again introducing local vegetation, controlling obtrusive species, and carrying out economical land the board rehearses are key parts of fruitful territory reclamation drives.

3. **Environment Versatile Protection Techniques**

As environmental change keeps on presenting difficulties, future preservation methodologies should be environment versatile. This includes recognizing and focusing on natural surroundings that are probably going to stay stable notwithstanding environment vacillations. Environment informed preservation arranging guarantees that endeavors are centered around regions where kangaroo populaces have the most obvious opportunity with regards to adjusting to changing ecological circumstances.

III. Maintainable Administration Practices

1. **Moral Populace The board**

   The eventual fate of kangaroo the board includes a change in perspective towards moral populace the executives. Executing accommodating and non-deadly techniques for populace control, for example, ripeness control measures and local area based approaches, can assist with addressing human-natural life clashes without depending on winnowing. Moral contemplations ought to direct choices on populace the executives to guarantee the prosperity of individual kangaroos.

2. **Local area Drove Protection Drives**

   Enabling neighborhood networks to play a functioning job in kangaroo preservation is a critical heading for what's to come. Local area drove drives, including resident science projects, environment rebuilding programs, and instructive missions, cultivate a feeling of obligation and commitment. This cooperative methodology reinforces the association among networks and the preservation of their nearby kangaroo populaces.

3. **Boosting Reasonable Land Practices**

To advance economical land rehearses that benefit kangaroo natural surroundings, future bearings ought to incorporate making impetuses for landowners. Monetary and non-monetary motivating forces, for example, tax reductions, preservation easements, or affirmation programs, can urge landowners to embrace rehearses that help kangaroo-accommodating scenes.

IV. Mechanical Advancements in Protection

1. **Remote Detecting and Observing Advancements**

   Headways in remote detecting and observing advancements offer promising roads for preservation. Satellite symbolism, robots, and sensor organizations can give continuous information on kangaroo territories, populace elements, and environment wellbeing. This innovation takes into account more exact protection arranging and works with quick reactions to arising dangers.

2. **Information Investigation for Protection Independent direction**

   The fate of kangaroo protection includes saddling the force of information investigation for informed direction. Breaking down huge datasets on kangaroo conduct, hereditary qualities, and biological associations can uncover examples and patterns that illuminate protection systems. AI calculations can help with anticipating populace elements, surveying natural surroundings quality, and streamlining protection mediations.

3. **Genomic Ways to deal with Protection**

Genomic advances offer additional opportunities for figuring out the hereditary variety and flexibility of kangaroo populaces. Incorporating genomics into preservation endeavors empowers researchers to evaluate the strength of populaces, recognize hereditarily unmistakable gatherings, and illuminate reproducing programs. This data is pivotal for keeping up with hereditary variety and strength notwithstanding natural changes.

V. Local area Commitment and Schooling

1. **Intuitive Instructive Projects**
   The fate of kangaroo protection incorporates dynamic and intuitive instructive projects. Augmented reality encounters, online stages, and vivid displays can draw in crowds in finding out about kangaroo conduct, biology, and protection challenges. These projects cultivate an association between general society and kangaroo protection, rousing a feeling of stewardship.

2. **Local area Science and Observing Projects**
   Local area science drives will assume an imperative part in checking kangaroo populaces. Resident science programs engage people to add to information assortment, populace observing, and environment appraisals. These cooperative endeavors make a feeling of shared liability and advance a more profound comprehension of the difficulties looked by kangaroos.

3. **Social Awareness in Protection Informing**

Future preservation drives should focus on social responsiveness and regard for assorted viewpoints. Teaming up with Native people group and incorporating customary natural information guarantees that protection endeavors line up with social qualities. Integrating social stories into protection informing encourages a more comprehensive and powerful way to deal with kangaroo preservation.

VI. Worldwide Joint effort for Preservation

1. **Global Protection Organizations**
   The fate of kangaroo protection lies in fortified worldwide associations. Co-operative drives between nations, preservation associations, and research organizations can work with the trading of information, assets, and best practices. Shared endeavors are especially urgent for transitory kangaroo species that navigate different nations.

2. **Preservation Strategy for Kangaroo Security**
   Participating in preservation tact is fundamental for upholding for kangaroo

assurance at the worldwide level. This includes conciliatory endeavors to bring issues to light about the preservation status of kangaroos, gather global help for their insurance, and address transboundary issues. Protection discretion adds to the improvement of strategies that focus on kangaroo preservation on a world-wide scale.

3. **Worldwide Preservation Financing for Kangaroo Drives**

Getting worldwide protection subsidizing is a vital future heading for kangaroo drives. Worldwide money sources, generous associations, and cooperative award projects can offer monetary help for research, preservation tasks, and local area commitment endeavors. This financing is basic for carrying out huge scope, effective protection procedures.

VII. Moral Contemplations in Bondage

1. **Headways in Hostage Conditions**
   For kangaroos in bondage, what's to come involves progressions in walled in area plan and farming practices. Establishing more naturalistic and enhancing conditions, tending to wellbeing and government assistance concerns, and advancing moral contemplations in hostage settings add to the prosperity of hostage kangaroo populaces.

2. **Preservation centered Hostage Rearing Projects**
   Hostage reproducing projects will keep on assuming a part in kangaroo protection. The emphasis ought to be on preservation arranged rearing projects that focus on hereditary variety, social uprightness, and the potential for future renewed introduction endeavors. These projects should line up with moral contemplations and government assistance norms.

3. **Public Commitment to Hostage Preservation**

Future bearings for hostage kangaroo protection include expanded public commitment. Zoos, safe-havens, and natural life parks can act as instructive centers, advancing mindfulness about kangaroo protection challenges and the significance of moral hostage the board. Straightforward correspondence with the public cultivates support for hostage preservation drives.

VIII. Preservation Through Ecotourism

1. **Advancing Mindful Untamed life The travel industry**
   Ecotourism holds potential as a preservation device when overseen mindfully. Future headings include advancing natural life the travel industry that focuses on the prosperity of kangaroos and their territories. Directed visits, instructive projects, and capable survey rehearses add to both protection subsidizing and public mindfulness.

2. Local area Based Ecotourism Drives

Connecting with nearby networks in ecotourism drives is a promising future course. Local area based ecotourism engages occupants to take part in and benefit from natural life the travel industry effectively. This approach adjusts monetary motivations to the preservation of kangaroo living spaces, cultivating a feeling of shared liability.

IX. Moral and Social Contemplations

1. Coordination of Native Information

The fate of kangaroo protection requests a more profound incorporation of Native information and viewpoints. Teaming up with Native people group, regarding customary biological information, and consolidating Native voices in dynamic cycles add to socially delicate and compelling preservation.

2. Offsetting Social Practices with Protection Objectives

Future endeavors should explore the fragile harmony between regarding social practices and accomplishing protection objectives. Working cooperatively with Native people group, moderates can find arrangements that line up with both social qualities and the basic to safeguard kangaroo populaces and their environments.

7.1 Advances in Captive Kangaroo Management

Hostage kangaroo the executives has seen huge progressions lately, determined by a developing accentuation on moral contemplations, government assistance norms, and preservation objectives. This investigation dives into the critical advances in the field, enveloping walled in area plan, farming practices, wellbeing and government assistance drives, and preservation centered reproducing programs. As zoos, safe-havens, and untamed life parks keep on developing their ways to deal with hostage kangaroo care, these advancements add to the prosperity of individual kangaroos and line up with more extensive preservation targets.

II. Nook Plan and Ecological Improvement

1. Naturalistic Nooks

Propels in hostage kangaroo the executives focus on the making of naturalistic nooks that imitate the kangaroos' wild environments. These fenced in areas, portrayed by open spaces, differed geology, and local vegetation, expect to furnish kangaroos with open doors for regular ways of behaving, for example, bouncing, brushing, and mingling. The shift from customary walled in areas to additional sweeping and complex conditions upgrades the mental prosperity of hostage kangaroos.

2. Intuitive and Enhancement Highlights

Imaginative fenced in area configuration consolidates intuitive and advancement elements to animate mental capacities and advance actual work. Highlights like riddle feeders, climbing structures, and tactile improvements empower regular ways of behaving and forestall fatigue. Improvement programs are custom fitted to the particular necessities of kangaroos, cultivating commitment and mental feeling.

3. **Revolution and Adaptability in Fenced in area Use**

Progressions in hostage the board incorporate the execution of rotational walled in area use. This technique includes intermittently turning kangaroos between various fenced in areas to give novel conditions and forestall adjustment. Revolution advances a more powerful and invigorating experience, intently lining up with the kangaroos' regular nature to investigate and adjust to differing scenes.

III. Cultivation Practices and Nourishment

1. **Species-Explicit Eating routine Preparation**
   A key development in kangaroo the board includes refining diet intends to all the more likely match the nourishing requirements of various kangaroo species. Species-explicit eating regimen arranging considers factors like age, sex, regenerative status, and individual medical issue. Nutritionists work intimately with veterinarians to make adjusted eats less that help ideal wellbeing and generation.

2. **Scrounging Open doors**
   Presenting scavenging valuable open doors is an outstanding improvement in kangaroo farming. This training includes dispersing food all through the nook, expecting kangaroos to participate in regular rummaging ways of behaving. Scrounging gives actual activity as well as adds to mental feeling and the declaration of species-commonplace ways of behaving.

3. **Social Preparation for Cultivation Strategies**

Progressions in social preparation methods add to pressure decrease during routine cultivation methodology. Kangaroos can be prepared to deliberately take part in exercises, for example, wellbeing checks, veterinary assessments, and prepping. Encouraging feedback techniques, like prizes for collaboration, improve the kangaroos' confidence in overseers and work with calm administration rehearses.

IV. Wellbeing and Government assistance Drives

1. **Thorough Wellbeing Observing**
   Progresses in veterinary consideration incorporate the execution of exhaustive wellbeing checking programs for hostage kangaroos. Customary wellbeing check-ups, blood examinations, and painless analytic methods add to early recognition of medical problems. Proactive wellbeing the executives takes into consideration opportune mediation and guarantees the general prosperity of individual kangaroos.

2. **Stress Decrease Techniques**

Hostage kangaroo the board currently accentuates pressure decrease procedures to improve government assistance. Limiting unsettling influences, giving detached resting regions, and utilizing encouraging feedback procedures add to pressure decrease. Natural changes, like visual hindrances and calm zones, make spaces where kangaroos can withdraw when they need a break from general visibility.

3. **Social Elements and Gathering Organization**

Understanding the social elements of kangaroos is urgent for advancing positive government assistance. Propels in hostage the executives include cautious thought of gathering sythesis, considering social designs, age, and similarity. Information on kangaroo social ways of behaving illuminates choices on gathering people, encouraging positive connections and diminishing the gamble of social pressure.

V. Protection Centered Hostage Reproducing Projects

1. **Hereditary Administration Methodologies**

Protection centered reproducing programs plan to keep up with hereditary variety inside hostage kangaroo populaces. Hereditary administration procedures include evaluating the relatedness of people, keeping away from inbreeding, and focusing on pairings that add to the generally hereditary wellbeing of the populace. Cooperative endeavors between establishments upgrade the adequacy of hereditary administration.

2. **Renewed introduction Conventions**

Propels in hostage reproducing reach out to the advancement of renewed introduction conventions. Establishments partaking in kangaroo reproducing programs make progress toward making conditions that get ready people for possible delivery into nature. This incorporates openness to common habitats, social molding, and appraisals of versatility to wild circumstances.

3. **Research on Regenerative Physiology**

Continuous investigation into kangaroo regenerative physiology illuminates hostage rearing projects. Figuring out the conceptive patterns of various species, improving rearing conventions, and addressing factors that impact regenerative achievement add to the supportability of hostage populaces. Research discoveries are applied to work on reproducing results and backing long haul protection objectives.

VI. Public Commitment and Instructive Drives

1. **Intelligent Instructive Stages**

Progressions in open commitment incorporate the formation of intelligent instructive stages that associate guests with hostage kangaroos. Computer generated reality encounters, live streaming, and online instructive assets give a more profound comprehension of kangaroo conduct, protection challenges, and the job of hostage the board in species safeguarding.

2. **Protection Informing and Promotion**

   Hostage kangaroo offices assume a functioning part in protection informing and promotion. Instructive projects feature the significance of kangaroo protection, the dangers looked by wild populaces, and the job of hostage offices in supporting more extensive preservation endeavors. Establishments effectively connect with guests in support drives and advance mindful untamed life stewardship.

3. **Straightforward Correspondence on Protection Difficulties**

A fundamental part of advances in open commitment is straightforward correspondence about protection challenges. Organizations transparently talk about the moral contemplations of imprisonment, the protection objectives of hostage reproducing programs, and the job of public help in adding to more extensive untamed life preservation drives. Straightforward correspondence cultivates trust and energizes guest association in protection endeavors.

VII. Mechanical Advancements in Hostage The board

1. **Distant Wellbeing Checking**

   Mechanical developments incorporate the utilization of far off wellbeing checking gadgets to follow the prosperity of hostage kangaroos. Wearable gadgets furnished with sensors can give continuous information on crucial signs, action levels, and personal conduct standards. This innovation empowers guardians and veterinarians to proactively screen kangaroo wellbeing.

2. **Social Examination and AI**

   Progresses in social examination and AI add to a more profound comprehension of kangaroo conduct in imprisonment. Examining tremendous datasets on ways of behaving, social connections, and inclinations considers the recognizable proof of individual necessities and the enhancement of farming practices. AI calculations can help with anticipating and tending to potential government assistance issues.

3. **Ecological Sensors for Living space Observing**

Integrating ecological sensors into hostage walled in areas empowers nonstop natural surroundings checking. Sensors measure boundaries like temperature, moistness, and vegetation quality, giving guardians bits of knowledge into the natural circumstances that influence kangaroo prosperity. Changes can be made progressively to advance the hostage climate.

VIII. Moral Contemplations and Future Headings

1. **Ceaseless Moral Reflection**
   Propels in hostage kangaroo the board include a pledge to persistent moral reflection. Establishments participate in continuous assessments of their works on, taking into account the effect on individual government assistance, preservation objectives, and moral contemplations. Moral systems develop, informed by new exploration discoveries, public information, and a devotion to further developing guidelines.
2. **Coordination of Partner Viewpoints**
   Future headings in hostage kangaroo the executives focus on the joining of partner viewpoints. Foundations effectively look for input from guests, neighborhood networks, protection associations, and Native gatherings. Comprehensive dynamic cycles guarantee that different points of view are viewed as in molding the moral and pragmatic parts of hostage kangaroo care.
3. **Worldwide Joint effort for Moral Norms**

Headways in moral contemplations include worldwide joint effort to lay out normalized rules for kangaroo the board. Foundations overall offer accepted procedures, take part in moral reviews, and add to the advancement of worldwide norms. Worldwide joint effort guarantees an aggregate obligation to moral kangaroo care and protection.

7.2 Integration of Technology in Captive Environments

The combination of innovation in hostage kangaroo conditions addresses a groundbreaking way to deal with upgrading government assistance, preservation, and logical comprehension. Lately, progressions in different advances have permitted hostage offices, like zoos and asylums, to establish seriously enhancing and versatile conditions for kangaroos. This investigation digs into key innovative applications, including sensor innovation, observing gadgets, augmented reality, and information examination, and their commitments to further developing the prosperity of hostage kangaroos and supporting protection objectives.

II. Sensor Innovation for Natural Observing

1. **Natural Sensors in Nooks**
   One of the huge headways in hostage kangaroo conditions is the coordination of ecological sensors. These sensors screen key boundaries like temperature, mugginess, and air quality inside nooks. Ongoing information assortment permits guardians to make brief acclimations to the climate, guaranteeing ideal circumstances for the prosperity of kangaroos.
2. **Vegetation Quality Evaluation**
   Ecological sensors can likewise be utilized to survey vegetation quality inside walled in areas. This is especially essential for herbivorous kangaroos, as it empowers guardians to screen the dietary benefit of the accessible vegetation.

Changes can then be made to the eating regimen or the acquaintance of strengthening feed with meet the particular dietary requirements of individual kangaroos.

3. **Conduct Investigation Through Sensor Information**

Sensor information is outfit for conduct investigation, giving bits of knowledge into the day to day exercises and inclinations of hostage kangaroos. By examining designs in development, taking care of ways of behaving, and social connections, overseers can acquire a more profound comprehension of individual requirements and by and large collective vibes. This data illuminates choices connected with fenced in area plan and the executives rehearses.

III. Wearable Gadgets for Wellbeing Checking

1. **Distant Wellbeing Observing Gadgets**
   Wearable gadgets furnished with sensors offer a non-meddlesome method for checking the strength of hostage kangaroos. These gadgets can follow indispensable signs, movement levels, and even rest designs. Distant wellbeing checking permits guardians and veterinarians to recognize early indications of medical problems, prompting more proactive and compelling medical services mediations.

2. **Feeling of anxiety Appraisal**
   The combination of wearable gadgets empowers the appraisal of feelings of anxiety in hostage kangaroos. Physiological markers, for example, pulse and cortisol levels, can be checked to measure the effect of different variables, including guest connections, fenced in area changes, or social elements. This data is important for carrying out pressure decrease systems and establishing a more helpful climate.

3. **Social Enhancement Input**

Wearable gadgets additionally work with criticism on the adequacy of conduct advancement exercises. By following reactions to advancement highlights, overseers can fit exercises to individual inclinations and enhance the improvement program. This customized approach adds to the psychological prosperity of kangaroos, forestalling fatigue and empowering normal ways of behaving.

IV. Computer generated Reality (VR) and Increased Reality (AR)

1. **Virtual Improvement Encounters**
   Computer generated Reality (VR) and Increased Reality (AR) advancements offer imaginative ways of giving enhancement encounters to hostage kangaroos. Virtual conditions can recreate normal scenes, permitting kangaroos to investigate and connect with virtual components. This not just adds a novel

and enhancing aspect to their current circumstance yet additionally invigorates mental and active work.

2. **Virtual Visits for Public Commitment**

Hostage offices influence VR and AR innovations to make virtual visits for public commitment. Guests can encounter kangaroo conditions in a virtual setting, acquiring experiences into the species' normal ways of behaving and the significance of protection. This not just upgrades the instructive worth of hostage offices yet additionally encourages a more profound association among guests and kangaroo preservation endeavors.

3. **Preparing and Conduct Molding**

VR and AR advances are utilized in the preparation and social molding of hostage kangaroos. Virtual improvements can be utilized to adapt kangaroos to novel circumstances or set them up for veterinary strategies. This approach diminishes pressure related with new encounters, improving the general prosperity of kangaroos in bondage.

V. Information Examination for Conduct Experiences

1. **Social Information Joining**

The combination of information examination devices considers a complete investigation of standards of conduct in hostage kangaroos. Social information, gathered from different sources like sensors and observational records, can be coordinated and examined to recognize patterns, inclinations, and expected stressors. This data guides proof based dynamic in hostage the board.

2. **Prescient Demonstrating for Government assistance Enhancement**

Information examination add to the improvement of prescient models for kangaroo government assistance enhancement. By recognizing relationships between's natural elements, social elements, and conduct pointers, guardians can expect potential government assistance challenges and proactively carry out measures to relieve them. This forward-looking methodology guarantees a more excellent of life for hostage kangaroos.

3. **Individualized Care Plans**

The experiences got from information investigation empower the making of individualized care plans for hostage kangaroos. By seeing every kangaroo's interesting conduct profile, inclinations, and wellbeing history, guardians can tailor the executives rehearses, advancement exercises, and dietary intends to upgrade the physical and mental prosperity of every person.

VI. Moral Contemplations in Mechanical Mix

1. **Protection and Social Perception**

   Moral contemplations assume a vital part in the coordination of innovation into hostage conditions. Protection concerns connected with social perception should be painstakingly tended to. Carrying out advances that regard the regular ways of behaving and individual inclinations of kangaroos is fundamental to guarantee that their security is kept up with even in mechanically improved conditions.

2. **Offsetting Mechanical Mediation with Normal Encounters**

   Keeping a harmony between mechanical intercession and it is central to give regular encounters. While innovation upgrades advancement and checking, it shouldn't supplant the significance of normal ways of behaving and associations. Moral joining includes insightful thought of how innovation can enhance, instead of supplant, the regular components of kangaroo conditions.

3. **Straightforwardness in Information Use**

Straightforwardness in the use of information gathered through mechanical applications is a moral goal. Clear correspondence with partners, including guardians, guests, and preservation associations, about the reason and ramifications of information assortment guarantees informed assent and assembles trust in the moral utilization of innovation in hostage conditions.

VII. Future Headings in Mechanical Coordination

1. **Headways in Wearable Innovation**

   The fate of mechanical reconciliation in hostage kangaroo conditions includes ceaseless progressions in wearable innovation. More modest, more modern gadgets with extra sensors and further developed battery duration will consider more itemized wellbeing checking and conduct experiences. Scaling down and improved usefulness will add to the inconspicuous and successful utilization of wearable gadgets.

2. **Developments in Virtual and Expanded Reality**

   Continuous advancements in Virtual and Expanded Reality advancements will offer additional opportunities for upgrading the encounters of the two kangaroos and guests. Further developed illustrations, intelligent components, and extended virtual conditions will give a more vivid and improving experience. These developments will be customized to meet the particular mental and tangible requirements of kangaroos.

3. **Reconciliation of Man-made brainpower (simulated intelligence)**

The coordination of Computerized reasoning (computer based intelligence) will assume an essential part in dissecting complex datasets and foreseeing standards of conduct. Computer based intelligence calculations can ceaselessly gain from social information, empowering overseers to get proactive experiences into the advancing requirements and inclinations of hostage kangaroos. This versatile methodology guarantees progressing government assistance enhancement.

7.3Balancing Conservation and Ethical Concerns

Offsetting protection goals with moral contemplations is a complex and nuanced challenge, particularly with regards to kangaroo the board. As guardians, specialists, and progressives pursue the conservation of kangaroo populaces, moral worries connected with imprisonment, government assistance, and human-natural life collaborations come to the front. Finding some kind of harmony between preservation objectives and moral contemplations is critical for the prosperity of individual kangaroos and the progress of more extensive protection drives.

Moral Contemplations in Kangaroo Preservation

1. **Hostage Conditions: Guaranteeing Prosperity**

   In imprisonment, moral worries spin around guaranteeing the prosperity of kangaroos. Fenced in area plan, enhancement projects, and medical services rehearses should focus on the physical and mental necessities of individual kangaroos. This includes giving more than adequate space, open doors for normal ways of behaving, and proactive wellbeing the board. Moral hostage the executives goes past protection objectives, perceiving the natural worth of every individual kangaroo's life.

2. **Human-Untamed life Struggle: Moral Alleviation**

   Protection endeavors frequently include tending to human-natural life clashes, where kangaroos infringe on metropolitan regions or rural grounds. Moral moderation procedures focus on non-deadly techniques, like living space alteration, fencing, and local area instruction. Regarding the independence and regular ways of behaving of kangaroos while executing others conscious obstructions guarantees an equilibrium that shields both human interests and kangaroo prosperity.

3. **Native Viewpoints: Social Awareness**

Moral contemplations reach out to recognizing and regarding Native points of view on kangaroo protection. Native people group frequently hold significant customary biological information and social associations with kangaroos. Teaming up with Native gatherings, integrating their points of view into protection designs, and regarding social practices add to a more moral and comprehensive methodology.

Preservation Objectives and Moral Quandaries

1. **Populace Control: Adjusting Numbers and Government assistance**

   One of the moral predicaments in kangaroo preservation includes populace control. While overseeing populace numbers is essential for environment wellbeing and forestalling overgrazing, moral contemplations become an integral factor. The winnowing of kangaroos as a populace control measure raises worries about the empathetic treatment of people. Moral other options, for example, fruitfulness control strategies, should be investigated to work out some kind of harmony between populace the board and the government assistance of kangaroos.

2. **Hostage Reproducing: Hereditary Variety and Conduct Uprightness**
Preservation centered hostage rearing projects intend to keep up with hereditary variety and social respectability. In any case, moral difficulties emerge in guaranteeing that rearing projects focus on the prosperity of people over the more extensive protection objectives. Finding some kind of harmony between hereditary variety, social wellbeing, and the potential for renewed introduction turns into a sensitive moral undertaking.

3. **The travel industry and Training: Mindful Commitment**

Protection drives frequently influence the travel industry and instructive projects to subsidize their endeavors. Nonetheless, moral worries emerge in guaranteeing that these exercises focus on the government assistance of hostage kangaroos. Mindful the travel industry rehearses, straightforward correspondence about hostage conditions, and instructive projects that encourage compassion and regard add to moral commitment with hostage kangaroos.

Systems for Adjusting Preservation and Morals

1. **Proof Based Direction**
Adjusting protection and moral worries requires proof based independent direction. Thorough examination into kangaroo conduct, nature, and the effect of protection mediations illuminates moral decisions. This approach guarantees that choices are grounded in logical information, adding to the prosperity of kangaroos while propelling preservation objectives.

2. **Partner Association and Straightforwardness**
Inclusivity and straightforwardness are key standards for accomplishing a harmony among preservation and morals. Including partners, including overseers, Native people group, preservation associations, and general society, in dynamic cycles encourages a common feeling of obligation. Straightforward correspondence about preservation methodologies, moral contemplations, and the difficulties confronted helps fabricate trust and understanding.

3. **Versatile Administration Methodologies**

Perceiving the unique idea of protection challenges, it is crucial for execute versatile administration systems. Customary evaluations of the viability of protection mediations, combined with changes in light of progressing checking and research, consider an adaptable and responsive methodology. This versatility guarantees that moral worries are constantly tended to in the developing setting of kangaroo the board.

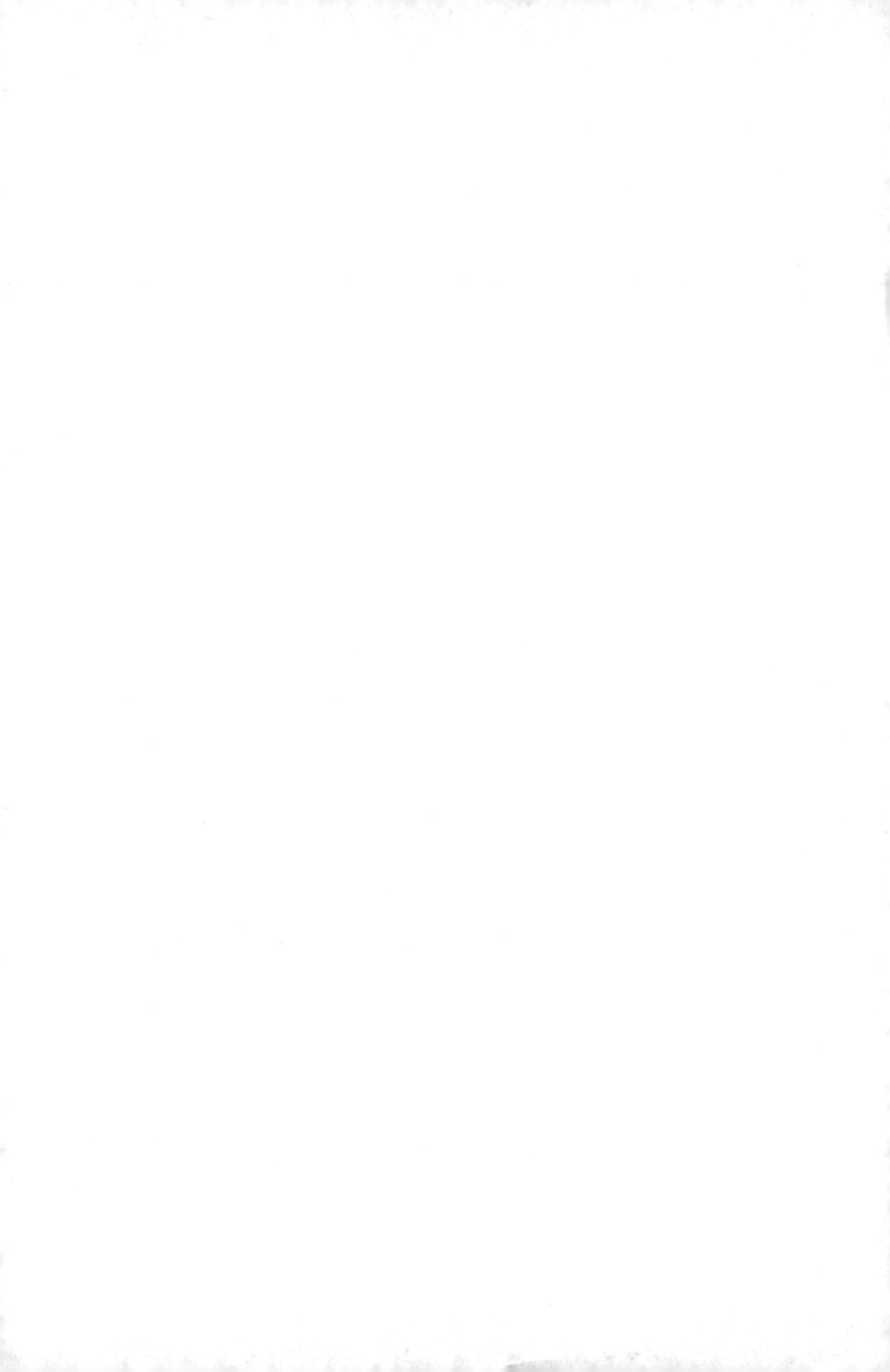